AGE O[illegible]L

A NEW WAY OF LIVING
FROM YOUR SOUL

AGE OF THE SOUL

A NEW WAY OF LIVING FROM YOUR SOUL

A MESSAGE TO YOU FROM GOD THROUGH

JASON NELSON

World Foundation Publishing

For information about special discounts for bulk purchases, contact: World Foundation Publishing, Inc. www.worldfoundationpublishing.com info@worldfoundationpublishing.com • Editor: Melissa Lilly • Jason's Teacher: Katherine (Kay) Beck (1920-2008) • Photo of Jason: Valerie Tabor Smith • Cover Design: Heart Centered Media

The author of this book does not dispense medical advice or prescribe the use of any technique as a form of treatment for physical, emotional, or medical problems without the advice of a physician, either directly or indirectly. The intent of the author is only to offer information of a general nature to help you in your quest for emotional and spiritual well-being. In the event you use any of the information in this book for yourself, which is your constitutional right, the author and the publisher assume no responsibility for your actions.

Library of Congress Cataloging-in-Publication Data

Nelson, Jason.
Age of the Soul: A New Way of Living from Your Soul / Jason Nelson.
p. cm.
ISBN: 978-0-9848285-6-2 (hardcover) -- ISBN: 978-0-9848285-5-5 (tradepaper) 1. New Thought. 2. Spirituality. 3. God—Miscellanea. 4. Spiritual life—Miscellanea. 5. Nelson, Jason. I. Title.

2013915744

Hardcover ISBN-13: 978-0-9848285-6-2
Tradepaper ISBN-13: 978-0-9848285-5-5
Digital eBook ISBN-13: 978-0-9848285-4-8

2nd edition, August 2013

Printed in the United States of America

ALSO BY JASON NELSON

Empower Our Children: God's Call to Parents, How to Heal Yourself and Your Children

More books to follow

Please visit:

www.JasonNelson.info

www.WorldFoundationPublishing.com

CONTENTS

Chapter 1

GOD'S INTRODUCTION: IT'S TIME FOR A CHANGE

I am the Source Of All Divinity . . . God. Your existence is so small in comparison to the vastness of Creation but also so *important*.

You are an advanced culture in many ways, and in others you have so far to go. When you look at the consciousness of people and the way they treat one another, you can obviously understand that there is a great change needed. But for now you find comfort and resolve in your day-to-day lives.

The entire reason that I am speaking with you is not by the choice of mine, but rather the choice of yours. If you were to look back on your life and ask yourself what you would change and describe those changes right now, you would see a great opportunity for growth. Still, so many people feel they are already living balanced, whole lives.

In reality most have no idea of the simple explanations that can turn your whole world around from *negative* actions to *positive* examples. But with every *change* there is a *commitment* to be *responsible* with its course. The change will obviously make your life different. This is scary for most people.

What will it take for your children to be given the same respect and love that I have given to you? There is no reason for the ugly pollution on your earthly home. If I were to walk amongst you, would you have me walk in polluted waters or breathe toxic air? The water and air were pure when you first inhabited this planet and it will be clear after you leave. But why must it be impure while you are here? Who has decided that?

Let me show you how you may live free from one another's fears and turmoil. The anxiety felt in this world is unparalleled to other civilizations on other planets throughout the Universe.

You have a basic understanding of things that benefit you and things that do not, which you have called *good* and *bad*, *positive* and *negative*, and *right* and *wrong*.

You have missed the most advanced understanding that lies within Creation. It is *unconditional love*. I do not suggest the airy-fairy concepts that your hopeful spiritual and religious movements have thought of as a clear understanding of love.

May I speak of love with the assumption you will consider it unconditional? There is only love with conditions and love without conditions. But love with conditions is not love, so I need not make the distinction. I will merely express myself with the expectation that you will be *open-minded* and *openhearted* to realize that there may be a *truth* about living that you have yet to find and understand.

The first most basic understanding is the universal *law of free will*. This is the fail-safe device created to give you the best chance of succeeding with your life's destiny. Whether you are a child or an adult, or whether you have murdered or saved lives, you are governed by the law of free will and there are no exceptions.

Because of this amazing governing rule of Creation, you have gotten your planet into many imbalanced experiences to the point of self-destructing more than one hundred times.

I agree with the majority of people on your world that there are choices, and people are violating other's choices every day. It goes much further than this. You are blindly, indiscriminately taking advantage of each other's *natural compassion* by manipulating the very experience that a human holds highest—*love*.

Love, mind you, is unconditional and is the basis for all universal laws. Those who choose to love unconditionally are doing their *highest* service to humanity. Those who take advantage of another's love through manipulation are doing their *lowest* service to humanity. What determines this is not my judgment or any wrath of a God. Rather, this simply comes from you. You, in the end of your life's journey, will tally up all the experiences you partook in while living, and through the process of evaluation, you will determine the suitable *balance* for your actions. This is called *cause and effect*. This is another universal law.

Instead of focusing on how to love one another, I will teach you how you may *love yourself*. By clearly loving yourself, you will be able to clearly love others. This means accepting every aspect of your emotional, mental, physical and spiritual experiences in your entire life and even beyond.

There is a team of *nonphysical beings* who is with you right now, assisting you with your trials in life and celebrating your accomplishments. This very guidance is the assistance responsible in those times of hurt and anger, when you felt as though there was no way out and miraculously there was an opening for you to retreat through. People who do not believe in this nonphysical assistance, will soon realize that there is indeed *life after death*, and this life after death is assisting them. How?

In the next century, you will witness amazing details of the larger plan meant to unfold within the next one thousand years. After this period of time, if you choose, you will be part of the biggest shift in the cosmos, well at least this part of the Universe.

There is much talk amongst spiritual and religious leaders about the *change* of this world, both physically and spiritually. But the change is not happening outside of you. The change is happening *within* you. Your perspective on living is changing. I will show you how to seize this change and become a role model for others.

God will once more give you the teachings, personally, that you must have in order to reach the true potential of the human species.

The human species is not the only animal in the cosmos that has beings, such as you, living in them. There are many planets with interesting forms of *vehicles* for your soul. It just so happens that you chose Earth and the human species for your vehicle. This means there is a really good reason for you being here, or else you wouldn't be here.

- I recommend for you to *search* your life for a good reason to be here, and then *commit* to it.

This is a discourse, if you will, on the evolution of Earth and humans from this point forward through the next one thousand years. After this evolutionary period, if you choose to incarnate on Earth, you will be born into a completely balanced world with no murder, hatred or corrupt governing bodies over countries that choose war over peace.

There are universal laws being broken every day by most people on the planet, and it is up to you, as an individual, to choose to combat this thinking with a *new way* of thinking. This *new thinking* must then be put into action and lived without denial of the *true self*, the *soul*. The soul is not going to leave your body, so get used to it being along for your life's journey. *Accept* and *embrace* your soul. There is no second path. The next one thousand years is the *Age of the Soul*, and its recognition must be bolstered or humanity will continue to suffer.

An engagement is happening that you, as a soul, agreed to at this time. This agreement is your participation in the evolution of *Earth's consciousness*. The perspective of Earth has been *unclear* or *colored* for so long that you doubt the ability of God to live amongst you. I have always been with you, and in this Age of the Soul, you will experience my presence more than ever.

Humans are to remember their direct connection with the Source . . . this change is to be celebrated. There has been much talk about a messiah or leader who will take this world back to the *natural rhythm* that it once had. There are reasons why God is interacting directly with humanity through these individuals, and I will share these reasons with you and describe them in detail.

First, recognize what part you are playing in my arrival. The personalities of your soul from past lifetimes on Earth have already refused my teachings many years ago, many times. But if you refuse them now, there will be a greater consequence than there was a thousand or two thousand years ago, because the affect of every choice on your life is much greater now.

My nature is not fear or judgment. My nature is Love. When you view *responsibility* and *truth* as *punishment* and *fear*, it is because your understanding is not clear. There is a covenant that I have with every soul to honor the free will and choices made therein by the soul. Therefore, you will not see me doing or saying anything that is in direct violation of a universal law, without the soul's consent.

Most people have little to no understanding of the soul because, as a planet, you have lived without the soul's wisdom for millennia. That is about to change very quickly, for time is not a luxury for you as it once was. As you realize your *true nature* and begin to live from your *soul*, I will have done my part in preparing you for the change that is upon this world.

You will be faced with a very responsible decision, one of great importance to your eternal soul. I will not make, nor can I make, the decision with you or for you. But I will help you be aware of the consequences of your decision. Choose to change, and you will be the role model that this world needs now more than ever.

I have been called *The God of Judgment*; however, it is not I who judge your life—but you. It is not I who suffer—but you. I will not create anything that you, as a soul, have not created. Therefore, I am not in a position to even bargain with you. I merely carry out the plan of your soul.

There is a *choice* being made in every moment of your life. You *feel* it when you tell someone you love them, and choose to accept them despite your differences. You *see* it when you are driving down the freeway, and there is a collision because someone chose to drink and drive. You *know* it when you are alone and feel alone without a sense of purpose and direction, and you choose life or you choose death.

There are instances where I am very patient, waiting for you to choose to change your ways, and there are instances where I am not. One instance is when I repeatedly show you how to change and become the peaceful, loving race of beings that you once were thousands of years ago, and you do nothing. I must validate the ones who say, "God has infinite patience." Yes . . . true. Also know, if it wasn't for God's direct push in your life, you would not be who you are today and might never make it back home to your Creator.

If there was no *challenge* or push, then there would be no *life*, and so you must be aware of the *balance* within God, for it is the balance that allows you to feel your unrealistic ideas of spirituality, God and unconditional love. These ideas must be grounded into reality.

Let me advise you now to help you in your soul's growth. At this time on Earth, you have a stronger experience of *consequence*, giving you the best *opportunity* you have ever known to successfully complete your soul's journey this lifetime. If you *embrace* this life, you can accomplish anything, and if you turn your awareness away from the opportunity, your lifespan will decrease and you will suffer.

It is important that I give you the raw truth, so that when you die and evaluate your physical life, I have given you the best opportunity to become the loving person that you intended to be. This is your chance to truly *rethink* your life, by using the perspectives and exercises in this book, so that you can fully take advantage of your part in this grand plan that is changing Earth's consciousness. It is my responsibility to make you aware of the changes and the role you may have within them. And if I do my job well enough, you will indeed seize the opportunity you have right now, and then have a celebration when you cross over to the Nonphysical Universe.

- I will teach you how to create *everlasting life* within you.

- I will give you tools to teach yourselves and children about living from *love*.

- I will empower you with the *uniqueness* that you have, and show you how to use it for the greatest benefit of all.

- I will *heal* you if you need healing, and show you how to give the gift of *miracles* to someone.

- I will show you *who you are* and how to become it.

- When we are done, you will never be the same soul. In fact, you will possibly *never need to return* to Earth to physically live.

- There are those who are here by choice and we call them the *chosen ones*. If you are one of these individuals, I will teach you how to *realize it* and what to do with it.

There are thousands of chosen people at this time who, by their kindness of giving *service* to Earth, *chose* to come down to help me in the evolution of this world.

- I will be more than happy to show you how to *communicate* directly with me, so you need no book or mouth of a teacher to show you the way.

- I will always be with you. From the first moment you chose to read this book, I am here with you. Stop . . . *feel me* . . . *invite me in* . . . I am all around you . . . and with love, I share my energy with you for whatever you may need.

- I will never leave your side, and you will be provided for.

➢ C*ommit* your life to God, and never question your commitment.

- Allow the breath of God to be with you always in everything you do, and always be *humble* enough to know that what I have given you is not of this world.

At the end of your life, you will become aware of all the choices you have made while living—some of which were overlooked while on Earth. Those of you that choose to become great leaders and play a significant part in the change that is among you will truly be given a *sacred teaching.* This teaching is when God comes directly to you and shows you a power that you have not known in a very long time. All have the ability to tap into this sacred teaching, though not everyone will obey the commandments, or rather universal laws, that govern these sacred teachings.

You will have a commitment to either *God* or *yourself*, and this very commitment will determine whether you receive the sacred teachings or do not.

The sacred teachings are sacred because they are received directly from the Source regarding your life. It would be inaccurate to say that you receive them only when you reach a certain soul evolution. In actuality, the teachings have nothing to do with your *soul destiny*, and are not even dependent on your *life destiny*. They are, however, very dependent on your *commitment* to your Source, and this will determine your openness to the teachings that will, for a fact, change your relationship with the world around you.

Some have said that giving up everything you have known for a new way of living is hard. Yes, it is. You will be challenged every step along the way until you break free from your *ego* or, in other words, leaving your soul and God out of the picture and decision making.

If you *include* God in and put God *first*, you will be shown things and given an opportunity unlike anything you have experienced in any lifetime you have ever lived.

Most of you have lived many lifetimes and are well on your way to completing your need for coming down to live physically. Others have a way to go.

You have asked the Source to come down to Earth and live physically with you to give you what you need to evolve out of the duality that the world has been in for many thousands of years. There is no need for the experience of *duality*, which is itself a burden to this planet. The only reason it exists is the many times you have questioned your *faith* in yourself, which disconnected you from your *truth* with me.

I have, time and time again, searched for a leader who would be capable of leading you out of the hard, dark times and into the light of the new, but have failed to find such a capable human being. There have been those humans who have tried and have done much to push you forward in a beneficial direction.

- This time will you embrace the leaders that come before you, or will you disregard the teachings and create a wall between what I bring to you and your families?

- Will you strengthen your ego by saying that the Divine would come to you differently than through such individuals?

- Will you disregard it as a trick created to try to mislead people further?

If you want to live in a more peaceful world, make an active decision to change the way you will approach the teachings once they finally reach you.

- Decide that your life will change, and it will change with each breath you take.

Create an opening within your mind and end suffering. If you do not, as this world moves more into the new way of living, you will suffer and eventually die because there will be nothing to support your unbending, egotistical way of thinking. You will deteriorate, as you are now, but at an alarming rate.

The human vehicle was created for a soul to have a *choice* whether it will age and how fast. Some have mastered this technique of *mind over matter* and lived for hundreds of years. The most amazing part of living from love, instead of ego, is that you will not have to die or age. There will be no need for food or water. You can, with the very power of your mind, create health or create food. You may also create the way in which you will experience everything and will no longer be *conditioned* by your mind to fear that which is unknown.

When you finally embrace the unknown, instead of fearing it, then you have moved into openness that I can work with. Because this is needed, I urge you to make your mind up now and choose to *embrace* your *life changing*. Embrace the fact that everyone and everything that you have always known is changing. If you are open to God and your soul, and embrace the change instead of pushing it away, you will be choosing life and live.

My intention is to follow the orders you have decided upon as a planet. You have chosen for me to come in this manner because you, as a soul group committed to evolving Earth, have seen no other alternative. If you continue as you have, your planet will be decimated with little to no possibility of rebuilding or sustaining human life. If this happens, you would have wasted a very precious opportunity.

I am here to carry out your orders stating that every human being, individually and collectively, as tribes and countries, must be accountable for their choices. I have also been asked by you, as a soul group, to continue with the plan no matter what. This means that your human personality may disagree with the approach and plan, but your soul has a higher decision that has already been made and cannot be changed.

Your planet, therefore, will *cleanse* itself for a *new generation* who will follow and put God as number one in their lives. This cleansing will happen much easier if your human personality agrees to it and *embraces* it. This cleansing has been felt and talked about for millennia. It is the great *shift of the ages* that will completely change the course of this world's growth. I am very appreciative that you have allowed and considered me to be the aspect of God that ushers in this new age. So, humbly, with all consideration and love . . . thank you.

Chapter 2

LOVE

Next time you incarnate on Earth, your soul will choose a life to receive the experiences it needs. This time around it chose your life to gain its desired experiences, and you must get used to it. Many people spend their entire lives trying to *escape* who they are, instead of *embracing* it.

To truly love yourself, *accept* your total life experience, including emotions and thoughts. If you do not, then you do not love yourself unconditionally. My purpose for being here on Earth is to impart to you the necessity of love and how to experience it.

Love is the energy of Creation and is the consistent creative force that never changes. From love comes everything, and to love everything returns. You experience something different than love in your life, only because your interpretation of life is unclear.

Your *perspective* of the world is unclear because you have learned this from your parents and teachers. Your friends and colleagues constantly reinforce an unclear perspective of love to you.

With *real* love there is no:

- Judgment
- Karma
- Evil
- Wrong-doing

If you believe and experience these qualities, it is because you have an unclear perspective of life.

I hope to reach the depths of your mind and allow you to understand how to live differently. I have gone from planet to planet reaching the minds of incarnated souls, and I have found one thing remains constant:

> When you look back on your life after you die, you will *cherish* the times you showed love, and you will *bal-*

ance the times you did not. This will never change and remains a constant between all souls incarnating across the entire Universe.

THREE ASPECTS OF ATTAINING LOVE EXERCISE

1. The First Aspect of Attaining Love:

   Identify how you perceive yourself.

   Increase your *awareness* of belief, faith, love and acceptance of yourself. You must first accomplish this, and it is the most difficult.

2. The Second Aspect of Attaining Love:

   Recognize your perspective of the world around you.

   Are you judging others or accepting others unconditionally?

   Do you *love all* of Creation or do you not?

   Creation includes everything, not just what you judge as deserving your attention. The importance of every human being is the same. The quality of life that every human deserves is the same. The love every human deserves is the same.

3. The Third Aspect of Attaining Love:

   Be open to the wants and desires you have.

   What are your *wants* and *desires* in their most basic form?

   How are they creating your life?

   Are you pleased with them?

With these three aspects of attaining a *love perspective*, you will have a process that can be used to change your experience of the world through changing yourself. Please understand it is you that requires change, nothing else. Allow the rest of Creation to tend to itself, and remember that you will affect all of Creation by changing your perspective of love. It is simple.

There are other tools that I will reveal, as this manuscript is completed, of how to look at a different world through different eyes. There are very practical reasons for changing your perspective.

Chapter 3

NATURAL COMMUNICATION

The most impacting way to speak is not with the words themselves, but by effectively *expressing* the *energy* behind the words. Because this world uses language so limitedly, I urge you to take advantage of another language system, before you move further away from *naturally communicating.*

There are countless ways for humans to communicate with one another. Using spoken words, only, is an unnatural, less effective way. Let me clarify. In the beginning of human history, there were no spoken words, though you uttered sounds that correlated with certain feelings. Thoughts were identified by *telepathy or thought transference,* which is a form of unspoken communication. The human, with its genius mind, has the capability to create a thought form system of communication that will replace the spoken word. It is a more evolved way of communicating.

Your teachers have taught that there are rules with language that dictate what you can and cannot do. This has limited the expression of humans greatly. There are, at this time, no cultures on Earth that use forms of communication other than spoken word as their primary way to communicate. In ancient times, there were tribes that uttered sounds that correlated more symbolically and were received with *intuition* rather than the physical ear. I will teach you how to use this form of communication, as some of you already are becoming acquainted with and using it without an awareness of doing so.

Expression is the essence of the soul. You, as a soul, are upon Earth to express your Divinity. You, as a soul, are a facet of God or Divinity. We call this a *divine spark*, and so you are an essence of God; however, you are not God. There is a huge difference between one who is of the *Source* and one who is of the *soul.*

Therefore, you may accurately say that God is here as a soul living a physical experience to express itself. *Self-expression* is the most important part of living and has been damaged by your civilization. Children are taught from the first breath of their little bodies to draw upon fear and cease or limit expression of their soul. This is at first a huge shock, but then turns into a coping mechanism that does not allow the soul to fully accomplish its goals on Earth.

So you have a rigorous challenge, being a soul that comes down to express itself only to be stifled by the consciousness of this world. In the end, your personality must strive toward remembering the natural self-expression that it had when it was first born into the world. This cycle is a root reason why this world has not evolved much in many thousands of years.

Understanding why a new way of expression is important is a key to changing this world's direction.

- Ask your children if they feel heard or if they feel understood.

- Do you feel understood?

You do not feel like anyone can fully understand you because you have an unevolved way of expressing yourself. If you were to embrace a new *expression*, or rather *communication*, you would indeed feel understood, and every child born to this world would also feel *heard* and *understood.* Wow! What a shift of life to have a form of spoken-written-intuitive communication that gives the soul a chance to fully express itself in the physical.

Language masters, it is up to you to get together with intuitive practitioners to learn and understand how to put both realms together and create a new way to communicate. This is absolutely one of the most vital paradigm shifts that is required to become an evolved civilization.

Children will then be born to a world that *empowers* the soul's expression and divine attributes, rather than punishing children for desiring natural tendencies of the soul. In essence, you have punished children for being who they are, and you think you are helping them in life.

Give children the freedom to express themselves, and understand this—your children are who you are. They come to this world to learn how to be a human being. You, as a parent, are their role model. They are studying you and taking on your thinking and emotions. They will become you whether you hide it or show it, because exactly who you are is what your children learn to become.

This is why you must love yourself—because the greatest *gift* you can give to your child is the experience of *loving yourself*. This will benefit them far greater than any money or success, as you see it. It will take them further on their soul's journey than any perfect relationship or job. In the end, it will be the only thing that keeps them from needing to come back to live physically. It has been a pleasure giving you insights on your children . . . I hope you consider these words.

The children are your hope and your future. They are the greatest investment that this world has. Choose well what you do with your investment, because you will be shaping and forming the generations to follow by your choices with the children of this world. It is imperative to reconsider love and your perspective on it. Thank you for giving me the opportunity to share with you about the children, for it is my privilege to take you through the steps of creating a better world for them.

> My time is limited with you and these words are to express *urgency*. When I reveal myself to you, you may require proof of my existence, and please know that I will not prove myself. I will come to you and share with you the truth of Creation, but there will be no magic acts to grab your attention. This time consider this book and your direct connection with me as the *magic* and *proof*, and begin to *act* on it because it is the way and it is the Light. If you are not interested in this *energy*, it would be a great service to humanity to give the book to someone who may be.

Chapter 4

FIVE ACCOMPLISHMENTS TO BECOMING ONE WITH YOUR SOUL

The human mind is the most advanced aspect of your physical living. It can overcome anything and create anything by a mere *thought*. All of what is happening in the world today is a creation of humans' thoughts—Everything.

I am interested in empowering you with the means to direct your thoughts and use your mind to blend into the natural order of living.

The Five Accomplishments, also called *The Five Steps to Becoming One with Your Soul*, is a unique, effective way for you to recognize and overcome any imbalances in your mind. Your mind is the *root* of all imbalances, and is creating most everything uncomfortable and unhealthy for you.

By understanding the mind's process and a means to clear your imbalanced thoughts:

1. You will have a clear perspective of love.

2. The world will change before your eyes.

3. Your abilities will increase as you clear your imbalances.

4. And as they do, you will understand the relationship you have with Me.

Balance is really meant as a metaphor, because you are already perfect. The perfection of your soul is reflected into the physical world, and so your physical life is as perfect as your eternal soul. Remember, all that is changing is your *perspective* of love. It is analogous to the windy or stormy day, how someone may see the day as pleasant and another see it as horrible. *Perspective* is the only difference.

Then, let me make the announcement that there is no *wrong*, *evil* or *negative*, just as there is no *right*, *good* or *positive* extreme.

There are *choices*, and those choices have *consequences*. If you judge choices, then you are experiencing the situation unclearly.

- Can you then view all experiences, thoughts, emotions and people as *neutral*?

If everything is neutral, then there is nothing to hate, fear or hide from.

This opens you up to *possibilities* that before were not present.

Chapter 5

ACCOMPLISHMENT ONE: GET GROUNDED

The first accomplishment is to be *grounded.* If you are not grounded, consciously, in your physical body, then you are missing something very important. You are missing your life experience. You, as a soul, came down to Earth to live physically, and if you are not grounded, then you are not accomplishing your objective.

To be grounded means that your mental, physical and emotional spaces are in balance enough to allow your personality's *consciousness energy* to be *present* and *fully in the body.*

Your *soul* is an energy which is not physical. Your *consciousness* is another energy which is physical. They are both fluid energies that can both be *in* or *out* of your body.

The *soul* will choose to always be *in your body*, unless the body is sleeping or possibly in a severe physical imbalance such as a coma or near death, then the soul can leave periodically.

The *consciousness* is your personality's point of power, and it will not have a clear power if it is not in the body. The consciousness has the option to be in or out of the body at will. This consciousness energy of your being is responsible for putting the mental, physical, emotional and soul energies together, which gives you the experience of life. The consciousness can opt to leave the body, usually due to a severe imbalance in the mental, emotional or physical spaces. Then you would need to find why and balance it so your consciousness may stay grounded in the body and operate your experience properly.

Otherwise, if you are not grounded, you will be missing valuable experiences that the soul needs, and the soul may need to experience them again either in this life or in a future lifetime. Therefore, you must be grounded to successfully complete your itinerary for your life's purpose. Through completely being grounded, your soul will take all the experiences you have back with it, and you will not have to redo anything. This is extremely important. You may only have an experience count if you are grounded, so master being grounded and hopefully teach it to others.

There are many reasons why you are not grounded. Most of the world is not completely grounded. If you are fifty percent grounded, your soul will choose to take back fifty percent of the experiences. If you are not grounded at all, your soul will take back no experiences, and you might say you are wasting your life opportunity.

There are some very prominent *symptoms* of being ungrounded which include:

- A *spacey* feeling. Your mind may drift around to *future* and *past* thoughts or visions.

- You may read something many times only to find that you have *not grasped* its contents.

- Your *energy* may be *extremes* of up and down, feeling tired or energetic, but rarely a consistent balanced energy.

- Someone can speak to an ungrounded person, and the person will seem *somewhere else* or *empty*, and even *emotionless*.

- You will develop physical, mental and emotional disease or illness as you call it, better referred to as *imbalance*.

When you are not grounded, you are not functioning properly, and as a result, you will suffer the consequences: physically, mentally and emotionally. Depending on the *root* of why you are not grounded, you will show different symptoms. The root will most likely be in the *mind.*

Physical imbalances in the body that may cause someone to be ungrounded include:

- Malnourishment
- Lack of exercise
- Lack of sleep
- Pain
- Overweight
- Underweight

Emotional imbalances may be so overwhelming that a human will want to escape them and consciously leave the *physical space* or *body*, which is where the emotions are felt. This is very common.

Mental imbalances causing one to unground would be thoughts, particularly of not accepting the self and wanting to hurt the self.

Sometimes a person is misled by a teacher to practice *out-of-body meditation* or *astral travel* through leaving the body. This is not recommended—ever—and is a direct violation of a universal law regarding being present for your soul's experience.

If you consciously leave your body, you are violating an even greater universal law than if you do it by indirect consequence of an imbalance that we have previously mentioned. Whether you are *consciously* or *subconsciously* leaving your body, it is violating very sacred laws that govern your soul's experience. You must consider this.

To ground yourself, first put your attention to being present for your soul's experience and *choose* to be grounded. You have an option to be present, which may be more challenging and real than to be ungrounded. But if you escape emotions, pain or anything else, know that these things will not disappear and will most likely intensify in strength and experience. There are so many people who never know what it is like to be fully grounded, because they have not even known they were ungrounded.

Share this vital information with everyone you know. It is the one thing that could save them lifetimes of returning and redoing the same things.

Being grounded is being present for all of your emotions, thoughts and physical experiences, including the imbalances. This means you must *accept* them all. To the degree you accept what is happening with you, is directly related to how grounded you will be. This creates a responsibility to be present for all the experiences you are creating, even if they are challenging for you. It is imperative that you accept all of your thoughts, emotions, feelings and physicality. Otherwise, you may not complete your soul's destiny and will return again and again, over and over.

TIPS TO HELP YOU GROUND

After you have chosen to accept all of yourself, you may use a necklace, other jewelry, or substance of a vibration that will ground your *field*, otherwise known as *aura* or *consciousness.*

This *vibration* will immediately pull your consciousness down into your body, provided it is the exact material that you need for your imbalance.

Otherwise, you may use a naturally occurring mineral or supplement to provide your body with sustenance that it may be lacking. Other dietary factors may apply.

Please note that these remedies are a bandage, of sorts, that will balance the problem while you are getting to the real root, which is most likely on a mental level. Please do not stop here but adhere to the full Five Accomplishments. If you stop here knowing that this is not the solution or root, you will be violating a universal law under *self-love* known as *self-preservation.*

- Proper *water* intake and *exercise* is important for every person every day.

- *Cleanliness* is also important.

- Enough *sleep* is important, which will depend on each person's life.

Sleep ranges between no less than 5 hours within 24 hours, to no more than 15 hours within 24 hours. Whether you are sick or healthy, you must follow these guidelines. Most will find a balanced sleep between 6 and 12 hours within 24 hours.

Even when you learn the teachings of agelessness and experience this, you will still require sleep. This is the one attribute of living that is essential, for it is in this space of life that you rejuvenate yourself by leaving your body and crossing to the *Nonphysical Universe* to replenish through direct contact with the Source Of All Divinity, which cannot be done any other way. If you do not sleep, you will die, and this falls under the universal *law of self-preservation.*

I will show you how to preserve your life so you may not have to age, but first, you must get grounded and clear through all of your mind's imbalances. All of the following are tools and are not to be a permanent way to ground. They are recourse while you are processing through your minds imbalances.

The more the systems of your body, mind and emotions are balanced the better.

- How is your temperature?
- Are your feet cold or hot?
- What is happening with you?

Love yourself enough to pay attention to the little things about how your body is doing, and be responsible to take care of and nurture yourself.

- When you are *nurturing* yourself, you become *grounded.*

- When you are *ignoring* your needs, you will become *ungrounded.*

It is simple.

GROUNDING EXERCISES

HAND CLASP GROUNDING EXERCISE

1. Do a handclasp, crisscrossing your fingers, as if you are praying.

2. Breathe in.

3. As you breathe out, squeeze your hands, and while doing so, imagine your consciousness moving down into your feet, even *feel* your feet. You want your consciousness to be fully grounded into your feet and beyond.

BREATH GROUNDING EXERCISE

1. Breathe deeply from your belly, visualizing your consciousness moving down into your feet and beyond.

Your breath must always come from the bottom of your belly, for if it comes from your chest, you may be in fear or out of your body to some degree.

SHOULDER CLASP GROUNDING EXERCISE

1. Put your left hand up on your right shoulder.

2. Cross your right arm over your left, and hold your left shoulder with your right hand.

3. Breathe in.

4. As you breathe out, squeeze your shoulders, and while doing so, imagine your consciousness moving down into your feet, even *feel* your feet. You want your consciousness to be fully grounded into your feet and beyond.

CHAKRAS

A *chakra* is an energetic experience that you are having physically. You might say they are explained as swirling energy-centers, for the purpose of meditation and grounding.

ASCENDING CHAKRA PLACEMENT

1. CHAKRA ONE is just below the base of the spine.

2. CHAKRA TWO is roughly two inches below the belly button.

3. CHAKRA THREE is about three inches above the belly button.

4. CHAKRA FOUR is directly over the center of the chest, at the heart level.

5. CHAKRA FIVE is directly over the Adam's apple of the throat.

6. CHAKRA SIX is centered between the eyebrows and about one half inch above them.

7. CHAKRA SEVEN is above the top of the head and slightly back, centered between the ears and about one inch above the head.

8. CHAKRA EIGHT is located about six inches back and six inches up from the seventh chakra. It is through this chakra that all higher communication from souls and the Source is transmitted.

9. CHAKRA NINE is straight up about four inches from that. It is where the soul lies and connects into your physical experience.

10. CHAKRA TEN is four inches above and three inches back from the ninth chakra and is where the Source comes through to participate with you in your physical experience.

There is an eleventh and twelfth chakra which, for most in this century, will not be attained. All of your chakras are essential for different aspects of your experience. In addition to the above chakras there are seven chakras that go downward between the legs, ending below the feet. To add to this, there are millions of chakras that affect these chakras. This will be talked about later. The point is that you may use the main chakras as *points of focus* for general clearing and grounding.

DESCENDING CHAKRA PLACEMENT

1. CHAKRA ONE going downward is the same as the first chakra going upward. It is located just below the base of the spine.

2. CHAKRA TWO is two and a half to three inches below one, or more with taller people.

3. CHAKRA THREE is about three inches above the top of the knee, or more if you are taller.

4. CHAKRA FOUR is at the base or bottom of the knee.

5. CHAKRA FIVE is one-third the way down between four and six.

6. CHAKRA SIX is where the bridge of the foot and the ankle meet. This is a very powerful chakra.

7. CHAKRA SEVEN is two inches below the feet.

CHAKRA PLACEMENT ILLUSTRATION

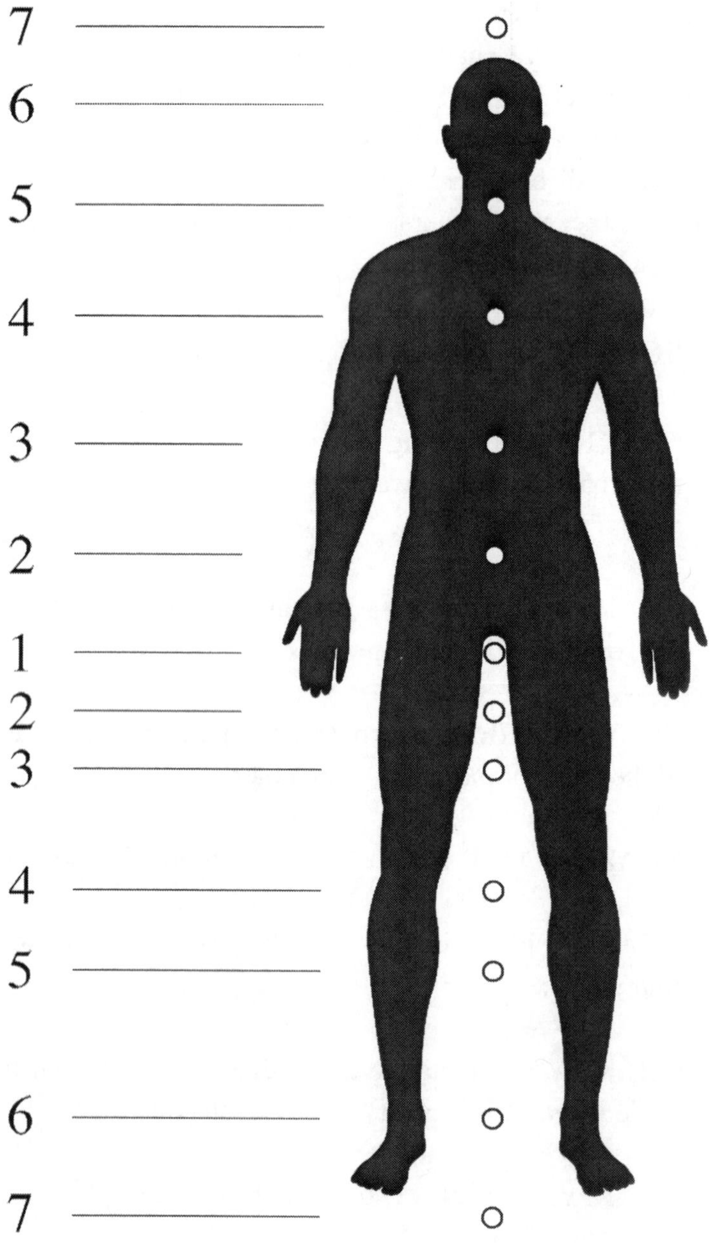

CHAKRA GROUNDING MEDITATION

1. Sit straight up and ignore what is happening around you.

2. Make sure that you are able to concentrate for about fifteen minutes.

3. Take a few deep breaths and focus on each of your chakras.

4. Spin each chakra as if there is a clock on your body over the chakra and the energy is moving in a clockwise direction.

5. Start by spinning the root or first chakra, and lead up to the seventh chakra.

6. Then, as you continue spinning them, go back down from the seventh to the first.

7. Now imagine seven chakras leading down between your legs that reach just below your feet, and spin those chakras until you reach the last one below your feet.

   Start with your first chakra as the first and the one just below your feet as number seven. This will ground you and clear you. If you had trouble with the other exercises, you will be able to use this and ground immediately.

The time taken to become fully grounded is important, because you cannot go on to accomplishment two until you have grounded yourself on accomplishment one. Once you are grounded, then you can move to step two and really be able to use it.

Chapter 6

ACCOMPLISHMENT TWO: GET REAL WITH YOUR LIFE

Accomplishment two is to get real with *what is happening in your life* and the world around you. Many times you find yourself escaping what is *actually happening.*

- An employee may know there are illegal acts or manipulation taking place at a company and refuse to acknowledge it for fear of change.
- The wife denies the husband is cheating, lying or raping the children.
- There are crimes taking place as people turn their backs and do not want to get involved, so they act as if the crime is not happening.

There are countless circumstances where humans turn the other way and act as though they did not see what has *really* happened. It is something that must stop.

You must face reality around you, and acknowledge its existence in every way. This means to accept it as *reality*, and make a choice of what you will do about it.

There is a huge difference between choosing to not take action when you are fully aware and facing the reality of a situation, and pretending the situation is not even occurring.

You must face reality.

I can help you to face reality. Call on me. I am the Source.

God is here for you always in whatever way you need, but you must believe it is so. I am personally going to give you special attention so you will feel or know my presence in your life immediately. I will speak about this further.

Chapter 7

ACCOMPLISHMENT THREE: GET REAL WITH YOUR INNER WORLD

Accomplishment three is to fully commit to *understanding and accepting your inner world.* Get real with who you are inside and accept it. It is imperative to accept *all* of your emotions and thoughts about every situation . . . though this is where you are blocked.

You have, instead, learned to accept some emotions but not others. Emotions are natural and are there for a reason. They are there to *indicate* to you something deeper that you need to look at. Whether you are feeling anger or sadness, happiness or joy, it must be *acknowledged* and *embraced.* Then, you may choose what to do about the emotions and thoughts. You may decide that they are benefiting you and not change them. You may also decide that you will change some of your thoughts and emotions to something else.

Remember that all thoughts and emotions are *neutral*, in reality, when experienced with a clear perspective. They are all giving you a piece of the puzzle to understanding who you are and eventually leading you to your soul's destiny.

It may seem like a lot of work to do everything I have mentioned. However, it is the only way. You will either do it now, or do it later; but eventually in some life, you will accomplish a pure, balanced perspective. It is the way to evolve.

Take a good look at the kind of madness, if you will, that is in this world. It is incredible how many people are angry and do not know why. Does that tell you something? Many people think that it is very normal to become angry if someone does something they disagree with, and in some cases they will physically harm the person they are in disagreement with.

It is a violation of a universal law to physically touch someone without the person's permission. This means that if someone calls you every name under the sun, including derogatory statements about close family or friends, you may not touch them physically without their permission. It is important to acknowledge this. It is not your right as a human to touch another without permission. The exception to this law is if your physical body is in jeopardy of being assaulted, then you must respond under the universal law of self-preservation.

It is also a violation of a universal law to express yourself to a person in such a manner as to manipulate that person. Many have *used people*, as you call it, and this is a huge violation of free will. So if your intention of expressing yourself verbally to someone is to get them to do something without their knowledge of it, you are violating a law of free will. You have a powerful mind and that mind can be used to control people, and if you choose to use your vehicle for such purposes, you will suffer severe consequences.

After getting real with your emotions and thoughts and accepting yourself completely, you must decide what you will do with your evaluation. My guess is that most will choose not to go through the challenge of changing their thoughts that are creating against what they really want to experience. This is because humans want to take an easy route. However, the road to evolution is directly through the fire, as you might say. Your soul did not come to Earth to skate by, per say. Your soul came down to experience the challenges that it created for itself.

The universal *law of self-acceptance* states that the personality must accept and take full responsibility for the life its soul chose, and live it out respectfully. This law is broken every day by most people, because their will to move through the torment of a day of challenge is short in most cases.

This law strengthens the drive of the personality to accomplish its soul's purpose. Even though most souls will choose challenging lives, because they evolve through challenge, the personality rarely encourages such aspirations of the soul. In fact, the personality in many cases wants to give up and forfeit the life, though this is rarely carried out. The forfeiting or suicide of a life is one of the most incredible disappointments of a soul's destiny. It is looked at as an anomaly in most cases, for under many universal laws it is not appropriate.

To understand the consequences of suicide, first understand something greater. There are at this time more than ten times the number of souls desiring and waiting to come to Earth to live physically than there are bodies. This means that you have wasted not only an opportunity for your soul, but at least ten others that were not permitted to come to Earth because of your life. If you consider the ramifications this holds, you will understand why the consequences of suicide are hard and impacting to your soul's destiny.

This connects to a greater universal *law of oneness*. This law is immutable and cannot be broken. You are one with every soul and every aspect of Creation. There is no separation, yet there is *identity*. You have individual identity, yet you are part of a great whole that is inseparable. Because of this, you are not only taking away from your soul's opportunity with suicide, but it is as if you are multiplying it more than ten times, by the other souls that were held back because of your life.

Many universal laws fall under the law of oneness such as self-love and all laws surrounding self-love. An aspect of this law states that because you are one with your fellow souls, by hurting them, or rather removing opportunity from them in any way, you would be hurting yourself. For instance, killing 1000 people would be like killing yourself 1000 fold. It is a very serious understanding that if grasped and acted on responsibly, will change the course of this planet. Love others, for they are, in fact, facets of Divinity just as you are, and they are one with you.

By unbalancing any aspect of Creation, and especially souls, you are unbalancing yourself.

Abide by the law of self-acceptance of your soul's choice to live as your personality. Honor and respect yourself. Love yourself. Accept all of your thoughts and emotions. Accept all of your experiences, including what you look like. If you have any physical abnormalities, accept and cherish them. For you, as a soul, did choose *everything*, except in rare instances. Overall, you can be certain that your soul chose your life and how it unfolded, and expects you to create an opportunity with every challenge that presents itself.

This world has built *coping mechanisms* to do the opposite of accepting. It is a universal law for the personality to accept itself in its entirety, and you must move toward this way of living. This means to accept the entire mental, emotional, physical and spiritual aspects of your total being.

If you cannot accept what is happening, either outside of you or inside, you need to use a modality of getting to the *root* of the imbalances and resolving it, or rather balancing it. There are countless ways that have been developed in the world to resolve imbalances in the four aspects of your total being, which I will call your *four quadrants*. The four quadrants are rooted in vibrations. This means all four vibrate at different rates, just as one musical instrument will vibrate differently than another.

THE FOUR QUADRANTS

The vibrational hierarchy is as follows from highest to lowest:

- Spiritual Quadrant (soul)
- Mental Quadrant (mind)
- Emotional Quadrant (emotions)
- Physical Quadrant (body)

Please note the spiritual quadrant is for the most part inactive in day-to-day life, observing but not always engaging in the personality's experiences. It is important for the soul aspect of the spiritual quadrant to be unobtrusive because it will take away from the free will of the personality if it gets too involved. The soul will impress and guide the mind . . . but never too much. As the personality becomes awakened to its soul, the mind will participate more with the soul, but the soul will rarely make the initiation. Rather, the initiation of direct working contact comes from the mind.

The balance that is hopefully achieved is the personality awakens to its eternal soul and chooses to participate on a practical working level, giving the soul an opportunity to steer the personality onto its destiny and more. For God or your soul to come to your aid, you need to first initiate clear contact. Under the law of free will, God will only in rare circumstances create known experiences with the personality without the personality initiating the contact. God, like the soul, is an observer, but when initiated will come to the aid of the personality and create an overall balance in whatever respect is needed.

The doorway to God is your soul, so experiencing the soul must first be mastered before any real consistent contact with the Source will be experienced. Remember that the ninth chakra is where the soul resides and connects to your physical experience. For God to come through the tenth chakra and participate with you in your physical experience, you must open your ninth chakra fully. This takes first, willingness, and second, a pure perspective on life. As you clear your mind and balance the other quadrants, you will open the chakra for the soul, and by doing so will eventually open up the chakra for God. You may experience God and participate with God, but you will not have solidity with that experience until the ninth and tenth chakras are completely open.

God coming through you invokes *healings* and sometimes *miracles.* It is up to you to be a willing participant with God and create the type of life that would most benefit your soul. I will explore ways to clear your quadrants in detail, but first let me go further to explain the innate nature of the soul and how it relates to your clearing.

The innate nature of the soul is clear love. Love, as I have explained, is complete acceptance without conditions of yourself and Creation. You may disagree, though your disagreement is not a judgment towards yourself or others. If it is, then you are experiencing an unclear perspective, and need to find the root so you may change it to clarity, or clear love.

Because everything is the love vibration, you will find that the only difference in experiences is your perspective of the situation. For instance, if you fear death and illness, you will attract the experience of death and illness to you. You may say this is a lower vibration than health and life, and yes it is, as everything retains individuality, but essentially under the law of oneness everything is also one. This means that you and every other aspect of Creation are one and are one vibration. However, there is the perspective that you are also individual. That perspective of individuality or separate vibrations is responsible for the evolution of Creation. In fact, all of Creation is one vibration. All of Creation came from the same and is the same. This describes the immutable law of oneness, because it is the very essence of existence. When we talk about different vibrations being *lower* or *higher*, please keep in mind the relation you have to everything else in Creation. There is a higher wisdom that cannot fully be realized while you are physically living. This is the best description I can give you at this time.

With this in mind, also understand that even though there is the perspective of different vibrations, all of the perspectives and vibrations are equal in importance. *Equality* is under the law of oneness. This is why all your emotions and thoughts are indeed equally important to you, and you should accept them all. This is called *loving yourself* and is needed to evolve. If you do not place more importance on any one of your emotions or thoughts, then you can honestly appreciate what they all have to offer you. Every thought and emotion you have is an opportunity showing you something, and if you choose, they can take you deeper to your clear self. This is why you must absolutely encourage children to express themselves and accept all of who they are.

When I speak of *importance* in this book, it does not mean that one thing is better than another. It simply means *pay attention.* You could call this way of speaking a dynamic attention getter, but whatever you choose will be equally of value to me. I will, with words, attempt to impress upon you that there is another option you may live by. Nevertheless, in the end, it is you who will discern what your choices meant, and how they will either support or inhibit your soul's destiny.

The idea of oneness is the governing vibration ushering in the Age of the Soul. The Age of the Soul simply means that every individual at this time in history has a unique opportunity to understand, connect and live from their soul. *Living from the soul* means that you will be living from clear love, the expression of your soul; whereas, the personality has experienced unclear love. When the personality and soul align, you will have an experience beyond your imagination. It is called the *Initiation of the Soul* and will be discussed later.

Clearing your quadrants is vital to your evolution. Let us start with the simple way to find root thoughts that are creating an imbalance. Also, understand that every *root thought* will have *root emotions* that will need attention.

1. To begin with, take several deep breaths from the bottom of your belly. Make sure you have accomplished grounding yourself.

2. If you haven't made it through accomplishment two, you need to face and get real with what is happening.

3. Then, use the Clearing Technique to identify and understand the root experience.

Recognition and acceptance of what is happening in your life is not an option. You must do it before you may go to the root of the experience. Not acknowledging its existence will block you from finding its root.

Getting real with your emotions and thoughts may take some persistent work, for many hide their emotions and thoughts, as we have previously explained. Also, it is common for one to talk their way out of accepting what they really feel and think. Historically, I have found that you create religious and spiritual dogmas, or rather concepts of how to be spiritual, and the very way you speak of them takes you away from your true, natural essence. By saying it is not spiritual to be angry or sad is nonsense. You must fully get real with all of who you are. Love yourself.

Make an intention for what you want to receive clarity on. If it is a situation, you may use the idea of creating a game of sorts to maintain a fun perspective on the clearing you are doing. So many times people place unneeded pressure and heaviness on themselves over evolving, and it really should be the other way around. When you are doing work to evolve yourself, become *excited* and *joyful*. You are moving up in vibration and clearing your perspective of life.

In your *subconscious mind* lies everything you have ever experienced. Even if you do not remember, it can be revealed. *Trust* that there is a *higher power* guiding you through the journey. Your intention is to find the root thought and the experience surrounding it and change it. The unclear view comes from a lack of expression or lack of acceptance for a particular situation, and results in what you presently are experiencing. In life there is only that which you learn and respond from. Everything is learned that you do, and if you learned it, you can unlearn it.

CLEARING TECHNIQUE

1. **Sit up or lie down and become very *present* and focused.**

2. **Focus on the *event* that you are uncomfortable with.**

3. **Get in touch with the *emotions* present** whether they are anger, jealousy, sadness, fear, joy, etc.

4. ***Open up* a space within you to *accept* what you are *feeling*.**

5. ***Breathe* with it.**

6. ***Let God come in* to move the emotion to the next emotion or thought.**

7. **Whatever you experience, be with it and intend to go deeper to the *root* of it.**

   You may go to a *vision* of the past or *remember* something you have forgotten, or you may only *feel* emotions.

   As you follow down perspectives, attitudes, emotions, thoughts and memories, you will be *revealing* more and more the *origin* of the situation you would like to change.

8. **At every level you go to, always create space to *accept* what is happening and *invite God in* to move the experience.**

9. **Imagine yourself *expanding* and creating more room for the experience to unfold.**

   Many times you limit the energy of an experience because you think it is not something that is benefiting you. Please change this thought. **Create more room for the experience, and *allow* it to fully express itself.**

10. Please be aware of universal laws such as not touching another or harming yourself, manipulation and things of that sort. **Short of violating universal laws please *express* how you *feel.***

There may be such a swell of emotion flooding in you that you feel overwhelmed. Please understand that this is normal when tapping into experiences that have been locked away. Once you give yourself permission to express yourself and that you are safe doing so, many things may happen.

Your personality may change. Please create room for this. If you want something to change, something is going to have to change. Your family and friends may notice you acting differently, so ask them to be patient with you while you are evolving into a new person. If your actions are unruly or your behavior is shockingly different in a disruptive way, please use precaution by distancing yourself away from them, especially children. Possibly children could stay with relatives while you are going through the purification process. It will disrupt your clearing process if you say "No" to what you are feeling such as anger or sadness. Once the process begins, it is imperative to continue it until completion, or at least until you reveal the origin of it. The most important point is to allow yourself to go through your periods of change, and if you cannot get away from the family, it is better to be a seemingly crazy person in their presence than not to evolve. Their soul understands and respects your evolution. Either way, you will notice changes primarily in your personality.

Finding the origin need only take several minutes or seconds if you are intuitive enough. Or if there are many emotions to release, it could take several hours. To carry on for days is not necessary and would mean you are not effectively finding the origin.

If you have trouble finding the root origin, then bring someone in to help you isolate the experiences and create an understanding of them from the teachings in this book.

Every experience has an understanding beneath it. Things don't happen *just because,* as many parents tell their children. Things do happen for a reason, and it is essential for the mind to understand why. When you were a child you could have felt your parents didn't pay attention to you or you may have felt unloved, neglected, physically or sexually abused. It is important for the mind to have solid understanding to be able to move on. That understanding is in this book.

If you do not find the understanding in this book, please share your questions with the organization that published this book, so that I may assist you through it and answer your questions through the next book, by phone or email.

By owning this book, you have not just entitled yourself to words on paper, you have engaged in an experience of evolution that I support unconditionally. You have my assistance.

The *origination* will most likely be found between birth and age six, where most humans create their basic personality. You will create your personality directly from the personality of your primary caretakers. Usually this is your mother and father. It matters not their title. It does matter if they were your primary caretakers. The origin may go further into adolescence or beyond.

A general understanding comes from the law that all benefits are mutual. The agreement that you created between you and your primary caretakers was done before you entered the physical world. Realize that you chose your parents and the experience surrounding your parents. As it goes, you would not choose parents that would not benefit you. Under the same law, they would not agree to have you as their child if it did not benefit them.

You are in an amazingly elaborate *play*, and it just so happens that you chose your personality as the main character in the play. You also chose the other personalities in your life like Mom and Dad to be in the play too. The point is that you chose the roles you are exposed to, and you are responsible for them.

Given the circumstances of Earth and the consciousness of most people, your soul understood before it incarnated that it would experience an unclear perspective of love during its lifetime. You can put this into perspective in every area of your life and especially with the caregivers that raised you. Your soul sees every experience as a great opportunity to evolve and gain wisdom. The soul will value every instance equally to grow, whether it is based on clear love or unclear love. What soul wants the experience of unclear love? Really souls are neutral on the matter because the soul's objective is to grow using the circumstances presented in any moment of its life. This growth can be done through either perspective of love.

Please understand that what you learned was most likely from your parents, and what they learned was from their parents. This is a history of learned behavior. You might call this learned behavior *stories* in the play.

You have the opportunity to change the story at any point, but most people think that they must live with their story and cannot change it. Empower yourself with the awareness that you may become anything you choose to become, and do anything you decide to do. Your life is your play, and you can recreate it any way that suits you.

Learn the tools of empowerment, and truly own the destiny of your life.

Please comprehend that every personality is doing the best they can with what they have. This is under the *law of equality*. Every soul is given the same opportunity to create a destiny as it sees fit. This also reflects your life on Earth. You have everything every other human has to complete your destiny.

Humans have created a *crutch* by validating and creating needs *outside* of themselves. Everything you need to start, proceed and complete your destiny was given to you at birth. Though you chose one part in your play and someone plays another part makes no difference in what is available to you for your evolution.

Your evolution is not based primarily on the material creations in your life, but rather on how you handle what is given to you. What you do with what you receive from life directly affects your soul's evolution. The big misconception on Earth is that your evolution is reflected in your material success, but it may have little to do with this. Primarily, it's how you work with what you have.

Therefore, it is imperative not to *judge* yourself or others based on material things or situations in life. For you did create your personality, and how you use what you created is what will matter most to your soul. In essence, you can appreciate that your caregivers are truly doing the best they can and did in raising you. The truth of your heart knows that you couldn't have done better than you did in your life. It is easy to regret and rethink situations and create doubt in yourself. The clear perspective is that you have done as well as you could have, and so has every other person, given what they had. Walk a step in another's shoes and you will understand this on a deeper level.

After you find the root of the experience you are working on, and get real with it in every way by allowing yourself to feel all thoughts and emotions surrounding it, **then you may use the understanding to balance it, and *change* the experience to something you really want.**

Remember to first allow yourself access to all thoughts and emotions surrounding the experience, and take as long as you need.

Some common *uncomfortable* emotions and thoughts that most everyone has experienced include:

- Not wanting to live
- Wishing a particular person would be hurt or die
- Anger, Hatred and Revenge
- Sadness, Jealousy and Fear
- Judgment and Blame
- Betrayal and Regret

The most important thing you can do for yourself is to first accept your emotions and thoughts and allow them to surface. Create a space for them, and allow God to move them.

The understanding comes after you give yourself space to be with the experience at hand. Through finding the root understanding of an experience, and then getting completely in touch with all emotions and thoughts surrounding it, you may use the understanding to balance the situation.

Many times the understanding of an experience has blocked people from going deep within the emotions and thoughts of the root. After entirely exploring the root, use understanding to quickly or slowly transform the thoughts and emotions into ones that you do want.

Give yourself *patience* . . . you deserve it.

And remember to *love yourself* as much as I love you . . . without conditions . . . with complete acceptance.

Whoever you choose to be . . . I will always be here for you 'til the end of your life and beyond.

Part of the whole picture is that you are going to have a different experience every time you go after the root. This is because you are always changing. Every moment in your life is different from every other, and every person is different from everyone else. So please do not judge your experience. Let your primal, raw, emotional and thought energy unfold and take its course. Only then may you go to step four.

Chapter 8

ACCOMPLISHMENT FOUR: GET REAL WITH GOD

Accomplishment four is the reality of God or *getting real with God.* It is absolutely the most important step, and if used properly, all patterns and emotions will immediately balance themselves, allowing you to experience the *Initiation of the Soul* or rather the *Initiation of Unconditional Love*.

The Initiation of the Soul is when you are truly coming from your soul's expression of love, and you are aligned with its purpose.

Let me clarify so you understand what, exactly, you are *getting real with.* When you ask for help or pray to God, what you are really doing is sending a *vibration* out to the closest vibration to receive it and respond. To go further, without making this too complicated, you are asking with your thoughts to create something and have your Source co-create it with you.

Fortunately the Source is everywhere, all the time, with all power to do anything, so you can be confident that your thoughts are recognized. But what assures you of that, and that your thoughts are indeed going to make a difference in your life or the world around you? This is one of the biggest questions relating to God.

- Does God *hear* me, and does God *answer* me?
- If God does answer me, how will I know?

I will clarify this the best I can.

I have spoken about everything as vibrations, and under the law of oneness there is really only one vibration. However, there is the perspective of individual vibrations that creates the experience of evolution. You want to evolve and grow and so does the Source. As you evolve, so does your soul's creator, the Source. God created the perspective of individualization so that God could learn from itself. At the same time, the Source kept its one identity under the law of oneness, which is what holds Creation together, and the *law of individual destiny* that all souls have, gives Creation the ability to evolve.

There are *three spaces of Creation*, as far as you need to be concerned about. They are the *Physical Universe*, *Nonphysical Universe*, and God or the *Source Universe*.

> The *Physical Universe* is the universe in which you live, governed by physical laws local to your part of the Universe and other laws pertaining to the entire Universe.
>
> The *Nonphysical Universe* is where your soul resides and where other souls reside. It is also where you work on your soul's destiny when you are not in a physical body. There is an enormous amount of information I will give to you regarding the Nonphysical Universe, but for now understand it as your home away from home.
>
> The *Source Universe* is your true home, where your soul was first birthed and where it will return once you complete your soul's destiny. There is a process of evolution before you finally return home to the Source, and then become the Source. When you do this, you retain your individual identity, and at the same time you are the Source of All Divinity.

There is a huge difference between a *soul* and the *Source*. You are talking about apples and oranges, very similar in many ways but also very different. The laws that govern the Source are different from those that you are governed by in the Physical and Nonphysical Universes, or what you could call *spaces*. In order to understand the laws that govern the Source, you would have to become the Source, and this is not possible until your soul's destiny is completed. Your soul will decide when that time has come.

You will instinctively know when you are ready to go home to the Source. What is this experience like? How do you know when you are thirsty? You just know. There is no experience you could ever encounter on Earth that would give you insight into this *merging* with the Source. It is your greatest elation multiplied thousands of times, and then you would barely have a clue.

Because I am the Source, understand that I can do anything.

Whether I will or not depends on many factors:

- Free will
- Commitment
- Love
- Destiny
- and many others

Primarily, it is your thoughts that create a wall between my participating with you on any level. You could say I wait patiently for you to choose me over the petty desires and wants of your personality so we may more actively co-create evolution. However, patience has been an understatement. You are sleepwalking around this planet. I have determined by the intentions you have sent me, including a better world, opportunity for your children, health, and survival of your Earth, that I will consciously co-create this with you.

I am here upon Earth with a power and experience that you have not known in many millennia. Announcement of my arrival has been echoing for decades. You need not fear . . . please . . . I am here because you have called on me. Underestimate your power as a soul and you will fail. Abide by the rules of this universe and you will live and take your soul to a new level of evolution. Let us then work together as we have many generations ago, and tithe your energy to the greater good of all. Together we will create peace, tranquility and harmony on Earth.

The unique *vibration* of God that I am transmitting through this reading experience simply means *safe*. It is to give you the empowerment of being safe. What do you need to be safe from? Nothing really, in the grand scheme of things, though you will understand when I say, you do not feel safe on Earth. So you have called in *energy* of God to create an experience of safety. I am a master of this, as far as God goes. *Safety* is something that comes from within you, motivated by a clear perspective, and I am here to show you how to experience it.

The soul has had a long history of believing that there would one day be a shift in the minds of humans to allow them to believe that they can feel safe with change. Safety is the key to change and is what I present to you in this book.

Safety does not mean that you will not die. It also does not mean that you will not have challenge or pain. What you will experience is a *peace inside* created from understanding and evolution that will indeed allow you to feel safe in your body's experience, every day and in every way. Isn't that something for you to look forward to? Isn't that an opportunity to seize?

A name cannot capture the true infinite nature of God. But names do serve a purpose in your civilization. What is a name really? It is a symbol caste forth which represents *energy*. Allow your mind to open up to the possibility that it is not the name you should be attached to, but discern the energy by its actions. What do I offer you, and where can I take you? How far do you want to go?

Your names limit you. The name of an individual limits the expression of the soul. It points the soul in a predetermined way and covets actions of the personality; however, it is useful for the primitive way you identify one another. Spoken word, as I have said, is limited. So then, please go beyond the name "God" or "Source" that I have given you, and seek my energy and actions, so you may connect with the true nature of my essence. I will heal you . . . answer you . . . direct you . . . and show you eternity. Let us begin.

Prostrate before the Source and give yourself in every way to the eternal. There is a Source in control of your soul and a soul in control of your personality. There is a higher awareness that you must be humble enough to give yourself to and have faith in. If you can truly give your wants and desires to your *higher self*, you will succeed.

So many will pray or perform an act for God out of desperation and fear. Let this not be the source of your connection, but rather let it be *love* from the depths of your life.

1. Say, "Not my will but your will God." Mean it—not out of fear but *out of love* for yourself.

2. *Believe* without a doubt that God can do anything and will.

3. *Know* that God will change your life, and *be open* to whatever the outcome is of God's changes.

4. *Give up your attachment* to the outcome of your life. Give it to me.

5. *Give your wants* and *desires* to me.

6. Please intend what you will, but then *let it go* and *allow me to co-create* it with you.

If you do not let go of the outcome, you are still holding on to control, and under the universal law of free will I cannot go against your mind. Truly give yourself and intentions to me, and I will carry them for you.

If you do not experience your intentions creating your life after this, then there is an attachment to be released. Most of the time you are unaware of the attachments, and so you will again go through the first three accomplishments until you are clear enough to absolutely let go and turn your life over to a higher power. Once you do, I can completely balance every imbalance in your mind and you will be free.

Chapter 9

ACCOMPLISHMENT FIVE: INITIATION OF THE SOUL

At some point you will reach a clarity that will change your entire life. This is when you move through accomplishment four and into five.

Accomplishment five is the *Initiation of Unconditional Love*, or simply called *The Initiation.* This is also referred to as the *Initiation of the Soul*, because it is in this moment that you have cleared enough to align your personality with your soul.

This rare occurrence will be seen more and more in the next century and will one day be common for every human. At this point, the Initiation of the Soul is rare and unheard of in most cases. To completely live from your soul's expression of love is an *honor* for your personality. It is a great virtue, and what every soul looks forward to, and what every personality should strive toward.

Because it is not common to live from the soul's expression of love there are few examples of it, but when you meet someone with this initiation you will know by being in their presence. It is an overwhelming sense of peace and love. The experience can be felt by even the most unclear of personalities and will change anyone who is in the direct vicinity of the person.

Everyone has energy around them, and someone with this initiation will have a stronger energy than the average person on Earth. The energy can change and heal just by being in it. There is much to teach about the affects of healing energy, and I will talk more about healing later in the book.

Last century there was more than a hundred people with this initiation, and now there are thousands. Ten years from now there will be hundreds of thousands, and by the turn of the century there will be millions. Eventually, every human will have this initiation.

In a natural, clear world, The Initiation happens at the end of adolescence after the human has achieved a pure perspective of how to live as a human. It is the final connection needed to carry out lessons and experiences in their lives. The human is designed to gain all necessary experiences in one lifetime, and this will happen again, when the world is in complete clarity.

How do you know when you are ready and experiencing The Initiation? It is initiated by your soul, not by anyone outside of you.

At the point of initiation, you could experience any number of things:

- A vision.
- Energy coming into your body and changing it completely.
- The voice of God or your other guidance.
- Even a trembling vibration in your body.
- You might just intuitively know that you have accomplished five.

It is not a small awareness like a butterfly landing on your shoulder or a blow of the wind. You will know obviously that you are different, and from that point forward you will never be the same.

Understand that once this really happens, it only happens once. You do not backslide. If you backslide, you have not accomplished five.

The orientation of accomplishment five is simple. You will no longer be directed by your *unclear perspective* or *ego*, as most have called it. You will be directed by *clear perspective* or *love*.

Remember that love is unconditional and is the vibration of all universal laws. By living from a love perspective, you are abiding by the universal laws that govern natural, clear living.

You will still be aware of the unclear experiences and perspectives happening in the world, but you will not choose to participate in them. Because of your clear love perspective, you will indeed be empowered over your life and will not be at the whim of the world around you. This very feat is what sages and masters throughout time have called *enlightenment*, *righteousness*, and in other words symbolizing a *highly evolved* person.

To put this further into perspective, refer to the biblical and religious texts throughout history. Even the legends have great use, as far as lessons and commandments to live by. Most of the people who have truly been an example for evolved living in your texts received The Initiation. It is not particular to one cult, religion or teaching. The Initiation is for everyone who chooses to do the work to be an example of love. The key here is being an *example*. An *evolved being* is not so by what they say or how they act in front of some people. An evolved being is so by the way they live every moment and breathe every breath. It is equally the actions as well as the process that goes on in their mind. When you meet this type of individual, you will know it.

When The Initiation happens:

- You will notice thoughts that you would normally react to come into your mind, and you will choose to participate with them or let them fly on by.
- You are no longer controlled by past experiences and people.
- The thoughts that made up your beliefs in the past have an active part in your life, only if you choose.
- It's now your choice to be angry or fearful.
- It is also your choice whether you will judge or be joyful.

It is true that you always had a choice in the matter, though your choices were controlled by your *unclear* perspective. While with The Initiation, your choices would be motivated by your *clear* perspective. Big difference!

Allow me to take you a step deeper into this. Your soul is love, as explained before. Your soul is the only authentic reference for your initiation. You can look outside of yourself to others to partly endure your required experiences, though your soul will show you much more than anything in your world will. That is the reason it is essential to get to know the essence of who you are at the deepest level. It is truly within you . . . the answers and teachings. You will need to formulate a clear enough perspective to go within by searching and extrapolating from the world outside. This is why getting real with the outside is accomplishment two, before going inside which is accomplishment three.

Many believe the sole answers are to go within. Yes, and if your perspective is not clear enough you will not be able to go very deep. Therefore, please value the external world for your clarity only until your perspective is so clear that you may truly experience The Initiation.

Understand that your spiritual quadrant is not something that makes sense, necessarily. As mentioned, it is a higher vibration than the mind. It is not of the mind. It is of the soul. You must recognize this when faithfully trusting your soul to guide you and take you into The Initiation.

What are qualities of love?

Giving for the sake of giving. You will give because the simple act of giving gives you pleasure, and not the outcome of the gift. Essentially, if you come from clear love and give someone a gift, it would matter not to you whether they broke it in front of you or cherished it. Your fulfillment would come from the fact that they received your gift and you were able to give it. This is true love . . . not based on favors or conditions . . . not based on attachments to an outcome. Remember to love yourself, and you will be able to love another.

Another aspect of love is *truth.* What is truth? Clear love. To lie or deceive someone intentionally is not love and is violating a universal law. A greater violation is to intentionally manipulate a person through the deception. You, as a soul, do have the prerogative to share or not share something, but to bare false witness is deception. To not share something is not deception. In a clear world it would matter not whether you share everything or not, because there would be no ego to offend or hurt. You see, the reason you have learned to lie is because you fear what another will think about you, mostly. In the case of manipulation, you fear the outcome of a situation and conclude that you must manipulate it to create a desired outcome, rather than being honest and clear.

More importantly is the intention behind the words and actions. Your thoughts are powerful and every thought creates.

I spoke about chakras as experiences you are having physically. In essence, chakras correlate to and are a way to describe an aspect of your physical experience. There are seven main chakras and other chakras above and below the body.

- Every thought is a chakra.
- Every emotion is also a chakra.
- Some chakras pertain to a combination of thoughts called a belief or a combination of emotions.

- Other chakras pertain to the physical body as a whole, or as its individual parts including atoms and organs.

- Chakras combine together, such as a grouping of thoughts, cells or emotions, and this shows you a different perspective of your experience.

Understanding that every aspect of your physical experience is a changeable energy is fascinating and empowering. You may very well create a *balance* immediately in yourself, and this you would call a *healing*.

1. You may intuitively tune into an organ chakra and read the energy to understand how clear or unclear the energy is.

   You could also tune into a thought or emotion and immediately find its origination, as in accomplishment three.

2. You could go further and *balance* it.

The very significant point is that every thought is creating. This means when you think from an unclear perspective you are creating your unclear perspective in life. You are to be very responsible not only for your actions and words but also for your thoughts. Imbalanced thoughts will create an unclear perspective on life and will manifest it for you. This is why it takes a degree of clarity with the mind, so you may access your spiritual quadrant and know your soul.

The soul will not easily be accessible, but the more you access the eternal part of you, the closer you will become an *initiate of love*. In the Age of the Soul, this next one thousand years, you will find more people removing things from their lives that are not in alignment with their soul's love. You may always go to the soul to know love. It is required to know the soul in order to know God.

Because the soul is not of the mind, you will struggle with your mind attempting to make sense of the seemingly senseless reasoning of the soul, such as giving for the sake of giving. Look at divorces and breakups of relationships in your world and you will see the most incredible struggle with love. To truly know yourself, watch how you have approached breakups. Individuals have really been challenged when it comes to a breakup. You might say that the personality's true colors come out during this trying time. If you achieve clear love during a breakup transition, you may very well be initiated or very close to The Initiation.

➢ Look to times when your love was challenged most, times when you felt you were taken advantage of, abused, abandoned or used. How did you handle the situation?

It is in these most trying situations that you must find courage. These instances are your greatest opportunities, for it is in this type of situation you may transition to love.

- If you are in a challenging situation, use The Five Accomplishments to gain a *clear* perspective.

- A more beneficial way would be to faithfully *trust* in your soul and God, and put the situation in their hands to balance.

- Take the responsibility out of your hands to balance another and *give it to God* to do.

- Ask and find the *lesson* for you regarding growth and *commit* to it.

The lesson will always lead you to love and the acceptance of clear love. This, of course, is from the soul and not of the mind. You will at some point turn it over to the soul from the mind and not need to make sense of it, as you might have in the past. Then you have truly transitioned.

If you have been initiated . . . congratulations! If not, please look to the next opportunity for evolving yourself.

The soul is an interesting vehicle for God to experience the Physical and Nonphysical Universes. The Source is a different Universe. Just as you have a vehicle like a car, truck, train or plane that allows your personality to have an experience that otherwise you would not, your soul has a vehicle called the human being. God has a vehicle called the soul. Understand what the soul is, exactly, so you can truly own it and become one with it. God partly experiences Creation through your soul, and your soul partly experiences Creation through your body. The use of these different vehicles gives another perspective of Creation.

God can come directly to you as I am now. Your soul can also guide you, just as your spirit guides, deceased loved ones, ancestors and soul mates do every day. You *always* have a form of guidance with you. You may not have an awareness of it, but regardless it is there guiding you. Most of you have many guides whose assistance is dependent on your destiny and position in it.

Without complicating matters, God and souls are present in your life in many other ways. God is coming to you in the form of a book right now. I come in many forms. You may see me in a sunset, hear me in a song, feel me in a kiss, see me in the eyes of your child, or know me in times of desperation and hardship. The Source is everything, everywhere and has all ability. Therefore, revere me in the flowers you see, as well as the darkness that comes at times . . . for I am everything.

A soul is of a different nature than the Source.

- There exist souls and the Source, and everything is created by either souls or the Source.

- There is nothing negative or evil created by souls or the Source.

- There is no power that has been created to oppose you on Earth by the Source or souls.

- The Source and souls are of pure *spiritual energy* and must abide by all universal laws. There is no option for a soul or the Source. They must abide by universal laws.

- Human personalities have the option with free will to obey universal laws or not obey them.

There is a *veil*, of sorts, drawn over the personality creating a great challenge for it to remember the nature of the soul and the Source. It is part of the evolution process. Because of the veil being drawn, there is the opportunity to take on and choose an unclear perspective. Because of this, human personalities have created incredibly complex laws and understandings about Creation.

- You have the idea that there is an equally powerful being as God who attempts to take you off path and test you to make you stronger and more successful in your evolution. This is inaccurate.

- You believe there are demons and beings that are real and may possess your body, making you do things against your will. This is also inaccurate.

Please know that any creation which exudes behaviors and personality that is inconsistent with clear love and universal laws is created by humans. The mind is powerful enough to create something that can truly have an effect on anyone who accepts it.

I repeat. There is no evil or opposition to God, souls or humans that is created by either God or souls. These things are created by humans and humans alone. To participate in such a creation by God or souls would be violating numerous universal laws, and neither God nor souls can do that or ever would.

The *possession* of a body by more than one soul is not possible. Only a soul can possess a body and only one soul at a time, by an immutable universal law. You may experience what feels like possession; however, actual possession is not possible. When a soul claims a body before birth it is respected by all souls.

When a thought is created, such as what you might call a negative spirit or demon, it will only have power that you create for it. If you know the creation can affect you, it will. If you believe it is out to get you, it will get you.

Let me explain a very serious, overlooked reality with children. Why is this society built upon fear and control? Your world is now, more than ever, involved in the most invasive campaign against clear love. If you observe the movies your children watch, even the earliest cartoons portray characters killing each other or hunting each other. Your adult movies are even worse. They are created with the very intention of scaring and threatening the safety that humans yearn for. Plots of television and movies involving massive disasters, war, fighting, manipulating, and killing to solve murder are unclear at best, and are completely and utterly corrupting this planets ability to reconstruct a clear perspective of love. The video games children are hypnotized with are programming into their minds actions and thoughts that are also unclear at best. If you as parents knew, truly, the extent of the programming by media and external sources, you would demand a change in this world. For your children's sake, please consider this.

You know and understand *positive affirmation*, as you call it. Repeatedly saying or writing statements like "I love myself, I accept myself, I am confident, and I seek a higher truth" is powerful.

Imagine sitting in front of a television for hours a day, like your children do, watching and embedding what you would call *negative affirmations*. Negative is just as powerful as positive, because in a clear perspective they are simply both neutral experiences.

God does not judge thoughts, but you must decide what thoughts you want for yourself and your children. There is practically no pure entertainment in the mainstream of media. What should you do? Be responsible as parents. This is a universal law that pertains to providing your children with the necessary experiences and environment to develop with a clear perspective, so that they might learn to make responsible, clear choices on their own.

The soul has a destiny that includes your physical lifetime. Your lifetime is only a very small part of the soul's destiny; however, depending on your choices, it could carry a heavier impact. The total sum of all physical lives lived by your soul are still just a part of the soul's journey, though a very important part.

Physical living is step one within a *seven step system* of your soul's destiny. Until you complete step one, you may not move past step five. You will *reincarnate*, or in other words keep living lifetimes on Earth, until you gather all necessary experiences to graduate from step one. You see, you may work on steps two through five while still on step one, but may not go further until one is completed. More will be said about steps two through eight later, eight being your mergence with the Source and what to expect with it. The soul has seven steps, and the steps go much further once you merge with your creator, the Source of All Divinity.

Your soul was created, or in other words birthed from the Source, with one, two or four other soul mates. Your *soul mates* carry an overall *soul destiny* together as well as their individual destinies. The birthing process is similar to physical birth in that there is a veil drawn at the moment of the soul's birth, creating greater challenge for its evolution. It is up to the soul, through gaining necessary experiences during its lengthy destiny, to grow and evolve into completion, whereby it is ready to merge back with that from which it came, the Source.

Soul mates, unlike many think, are partners in a familial way, rather than in the intimate lovers' way as is commonly thought. Your soul mates support one another throughout their life destinies and soul destinies until all are ready to merge with the Source. One soul mate may not merge back with the Source without the others. It is law. Your soul mates may or may not physically live with you during most lifetimes, and that is dependent completely on the life destiny and how the soul mate may benefit itself and you best.

If a soul mate comes to Earth to physically live with you, it does not mean you must marry them or even be intimate with them. You will most likely choose to have a balanced experience with them in some way. This could take many forms.

Please look at relationships from a higher perspective. I speak of romantic and platonic relationships. What is best for you, as individuals in the relationship, is where your intention must be. Humans are consistently looking for *the one* they are meant to be with. Know that if you are meant to be with someone, your guidance will bring that person into your life at the proper time. You exhaust much energy building expectations and searching for the perfect person. In the process of such exploration, you may overlook the one thing you are meant to be present with.

Your soul has within it everything to start, proceed and complete its destiny. Within your soul are the combined experiences from every lifetime you have ever lived. You might say instead of a record keeper, your soul is an absorbing, expanding wisdom. It absorbs the experiences from lifetimes creating a greater wisdom within the perspective of the soul. This wisdom is complete at some point and the soul returns with its experiences to add to the Source.

When you communicate through your intuition to the Source and other souls, understand what you are doing. For instance, if you speak with your deceased grandmother, you are speaking with a facet of her soul, not the soul itself. The soul creates a personality of the lifetime it lived as your grandmother to better relate with you. It does this by pulling the information both from its soul and from the records in the Nonphysical Universe. Every single experience, word, thought and action is recorded in Creation. Your grandmother's soul might pull the information of its lifetime from these records in addition to its soul.

Think about it this way. If you were in a play and played a character, after the play, you might learn something from the character but would take the mask and clothes off and prepare for the next play and next character. If someone asked you to play that character again, you may be able to do it immediately, or you may have to go back and look over your lines and find the costume and mask. This is analogous to when a soul retakes a personality to interact with you. If you were to communicate with the soul itself, it would not have a form or specific personality as you've known. It would be a pure expression of love with wisdom in one or many specific areas such as healing, love, history, religion, science or the arts. Therefore, all knowledge and wisdom is available to any being through the records, or by asking a being that has wisdom in the area in question.

A soul chooses a major area of interest before choosing its first life and that area of interest becomes its specialty. Then every lifetime and nonphysical experience will have a theme associated with that specialty. This is why different guides will be with you at different points in your life, depending on what you are mastering in the physical. Some guides are with you your entire life; others are with you for short durations. This is beneficial, as it gives the soul the opportunity to learn from those who have mastered the area that is challenging the soul.

Physical *death* is as beautiful a process for the soul as physical *birth*. They are the same experience, or at least very similar. Death is a birth back into the Nonphysical Universe. It is really to be celebrated, but instead many feel a loss, for they have lost the meaning of life. People latch deeply into the physical, hoping there is more, but not realizing the reality of the continuity of life. The *continuity of life* states that you, the eternal soul, will always exist. This law states there is no way a soul can be punished or banished, and that it is solely responsible for its destiny.

It is empowering when you realize the true nature of the continuity of life. If you physically die there is another great journey ahead, and it will continue to go on forever. It never stops. You never cease to exist. You have as many lifetimes as you need to complete your objective, and there is no judgment ever placed upon you. This safety net, hopefully, gives you comfort as you look at the road ahead. You cannot fail. It is impossible. In every soul and in God's perspective, you will always succeed and you will always live.

The soul's expression will inspire you, motivate you, challenge you and love you. There are some very prominent attributes that will be experienced when you are initiated or are getting in touch with your soul.

Until you are initiated, you will not have a consistent oneness with your soul's love, but you will experience brief or longer moments of it. These moments of oneness with your soul typically happen when you are clear emotionally, mentally and physically, and invite the experience of God in. The Source will come to you, and it is up to you how you will receive the Source.

When you experience the Source, you can mostly guarantee that your personality is aligned with your soul. Some will notice this alignment in meditation, prayer, holding a loved one, being in nature, or when nurturing yourself. Typically this soul oneness is not felt in the busyness of living, when you are with groups of people, at work, or even in the company of friends and family.

The important point is vibrations will affect you. While you are clearing yourself with The Five Accomplishments, you must set aside time and minimize experiences that will bring out your imbalances. Instead, be in situations that will bring out your soul's expression. What do I mean exactly by this? If your spouse does not understand the clearing you choose to go through, they also may not be a support for you. The things within you that require clarity will be affected by the things in others. So if you are still on your path of The Five Accomplishments, you will be affected by other's imbalances directly related to how they are like your own. You notice how some things bother you, some don't. The things that bother you are creating an opportunity for you to clear your perspective. Other people bringing up your *stuff* can be looked at as an opportunity, if it is done at a pace that is beneficial for your clearing work.

1. Know the soul, so you have a target to move toward. The more you can bring yourself into the soul space, the better.

2. Then, at a pace that works for you, allow your *stuff* to come up, so you may use The Five Accomplishments to clear your perspective on it.

Through experiencing your soul, you will know when you have cleared something and when you have not. It will be a reference for you.

- The more you clear, the more often you will be aligned with and experience your soul's love.

- You will also be able to take with you and hold the alignment in places and situations that you otherwise would not have.

- You will know your evolution and your closeness to The Initiation by how often you are in the alignment and how long it lasts.

- Look at experiences that would have *pushed your buttons* and created a *reaction* from you in the past, and determine if you have cleared your perspective on them.

Remember, the world is an opportunity for you to evolve in every way . . . please look at it this way . . . and nothing will stop you . . . ever!

The tools you have are widely accepted tools throughout the Universe and have changed planets around completely. I have worked with many civilizations similar to yours in evolution. Some are less evolved. Some are more evolved. With all of my work in the Universe, I have noticed one thing that will always remain the same—for you to be comfortable to move forward and evolve, you must feel SAFE.

I am with you on your journey . . . I will never leave your side . . . you have my guidance always . . . you are safe.

Be part of the change upon your world. Live truly. Be free. Die free. Regret nothing. And you will always move forward.

From love you came . . . and to love you return. It is your choice when.

Chapter 10

GROUPS

Working hard toward goals together is an accomplishment in itself. You are a *social being*, which means you are not meant to live alone. You are meant to have individuality and to *evolve together* with other humans.

Take advantage of the opportunity to work together and help one another evolve. Form groups. You could call them *clearing groups* to support one another through the process of clearing.

Forming groups should be a *priority* for everyone on some level. If it is not, then you do not love yourself and are violating universal laws. When I speak of violating universal laws, please do not feel as though you will be punished, by any means. A violation of a law is your choice and your soul decides, in most cases, what the balance will be. There will always be a balance under the *law of cause and effect*. However, it is an experience of *joy* and *opportunity*, and not one of *punishment* or *regret*.

As social beings, you must *work together* for a greater goal than simply that of your life. By coming together in every way, you will create change, and thereby will serve yourself because you are part of the whole. The whole is directly affecting your evolution each lifetime. Your soul wants others to grow under the law of oneness. In fact, you will evolve quicker if you are born to an evolved world.

So please consider group effort. Balancing your individual life destiny and the collective destiny of the group of souls you chose to participate with in this life, on both a small and large scale, is a great accomplishment. It is needed to evolve your planet and soul.

> A *small-scale group destiny* could be for a family, friend, religious group or work group, with interaction between members.

> A *large-scale group destiny* could be for a tribe, city, state, country or world group, with less interaction between members.

Group philosophy is something deserving change, especially the coordination of a person's destiny within the destiny of the group. You must reconstruct this approach before a clear perspective of love is reached.

In any group, it is essential to operate under the universal laws of equality and self-acceptance for your soul's choice of a personality. Under equality you must have a truly pure democratic system where one person's choice is no more important than another person.

No one is to be shown favoritism, per say. There are those who you will be interested in due to the similarities within your personalities. Still, there will be a far greater truth of equality beyond this interest. This means that the uniqueness of every person is respected equally, and under the law of oneness, you respect the other person because they are one with you. In essence, every member of the group, despite even the greatest disagreements, will support and respect one another, as they would love themselves. Under the *law of independence*, which states that all souls have an individual destiny and perspective, people will have greater wisdom in some areas of study than others. You will honor them for their wisdom, but not fear it, and will indeed see them as an *equal* no matter what their status is. They in turn will see you as an equal. The homeless person and the president of a country can share a mutual respect for one another and support one another for the evolution of the group.

Many people in group situations find reasons to go against the grain due to the inability of the group to function properly. The philosophy behind groups is unclear and deserves immediate attention. Under the greater law of self-acceptance, meaning the acceptance of the personality and the life your soul chose, you will respect the opportunity of being in a group, be it family, career or country, and make the most out of the experience. Constructive criticism in a group is important and necessary. This is, in effect, speaking your truth. The biggest distortion in group philosophy pertains to respecting another's truth and sharing your truth constructively. By constructively I mean clearly from love. There is no place for power trips of the ego or manipulation by position. The president of the company should deserve the same respect as the secretary. The children deserve the same respect as the parents.

Respect is not to be based on color, age, criminal history, religion or status. It is to be based on the soul inside the human. For if you don't, you are blaspheming yourself under the law of oneness.

If someone does not respect you, it is your choice what to do about it. In a pure perspective, you would share your truth with them clearly, and take a personal action that does not endanger them or affect them in an unbalanced way. If you participate in revenge, or something of the sort, you are not only unbalancing them but also yourself. This falls under the law of oneness and self-love. If they are endangering your body, then you must take action under the law of self-preservation. There are exceptions.

One who perceives and acts from love will diffuse situations as fast as they happen, and in most cases they will not happen. If there are situations happening with you that bring you discomfort, then there is clearing work for you to do on yourself. Remember, you are responsible for how you perceive and respond in this world. If others in your group are reacting from an unclear perspective, you might be happy for them, just as you would be joyful if they were experiencing clarity.

All experiences are *neutral*.

1. Do not feed other's fear and anger by taking responsibility for them to make them feel better.

2. Simply share clear truth and love, and let go of trying to change another person.

Compassion is the heart of the soul. Some misunderstand the nature of compassion. Compassion in its clear expression is honoring God within all of life, under the law of oneness. Compassion is an evolved experience because to receive it you must be able to give it. It is not something that is to be turned on and off. It is like love, wherein you either are showing it or you are not. Clear compassion, most likely, will not happen until The Initiation, for it is the experience of oneness on the greatest level. Then you may have compassion all the time, for the trees, the water, other humans, and all of Creation.

This honoring of God in everything is the height of love.

Compassion is not attachment, as often thought. People attach into other's experiences to try to understand another's experience. It is not required for you to be sad or angry for or with a person. It is not necessary for you to try to change or figure anyone out because you can't. Every person has a perspective all their own which no other can completely understand. Under the law of free will, do not try to change anyone. Let others be responsible for themselves and you for yourself.

The most important aspect of groups is that even if the majority does not agree with your perspective, you still *support the majority* with love. This is what your laws are built upon. This is the essence of *democracy*.

Chapter 11

PROCREATION, SEX AND ABORTION

When faced with the responsibility of creating life for a soul to possess and live in, there are many misunderstood natural laws to consider. Most parents have an unclear perspective of raising children; therefore, by understanding the *natural process* of bringing a soul into the world, you will give the soul the best chance to succeed.

Firstly, let me discuss *abortion.* A woman and a man may choose to abort the life that they have created. The choice is made by both and decided ultimately by the woman who is carrying the child. Please remember, the law of free will supersedes most other universal laws. Even so, it is important to be mindful of your choices and the consequences they will have on your life.

Until the age of about six months, the new life carried by the mother has no real obligation to a soul that might be interested in it. But after that time, the mother must recognize that the life she has created is required to house a soul. Sometime thereafter, a soul will lay claim to the body and expect to enter it.

There are countless laws that surround sex and the creation of life, but I will not go into depth on them at this time. Many have felt as though sex is the natural course of humans. Sex can be experienced in both balanced and imbalanced ways.

For pleasure, only, sex is no more than an attachment such as tobacco or recreational drug use. On the other hand, sex for the purpose of creating life is an *honor*, and is to be explored with interest.

In this time you, as a civilization, are prostituting yourselves in most relationships. You manipulate with sex. You avenge each other with sex. You misuse the most sacred experience humans have against one another for self-motivated purposes.

Your intentions surrounding sex must be for *service* to the Source by creating a life for a soul to use. Creating life can be the closest experience to God you will ever know in the physical, if you do it clearly.

More people are realizing the validity in *sacred sex* for the use of procreation only. This stirs up a huge controversy, considering your civilization has built itself largely on the exploitation of sex.

The reason you are not appreciating sex as it is meant to be experienced is the turmoil within you right now. Many use sex as an escape, others as a way to fulfill an unexpressed part of themselves. Clearly there is no wrong way to have sex. However, there are laws that govern its natural expression.

The clear expression of sex is to be done monogamously, as humans are monogamous beings, and heterosexually with the opposite sex, meaning male with female or female with male. Male with male or female with female is not a clear expression of sex, for there is no possibility of procreating. Therefore, homosexual sex is done for self-interested pleasure alone, and not for the purpose of procreation. This violates the natural laws of procreation.

An imbalance in group thought creates imbalanced actions in individuals. Please be advised that judging another's choices does not benefit you. You are really judging yourself and attempting to hide your fears and imbalances. For if you are truly accepting of yourself, you will project this by truly accepting others.

If you are on the verge of procreating or at least planning this, you must take some things into consideration. Most importantly is the universal *law of the biological parents' responsibility*. You are, by this law, responsible for any life that you create. It goes on to state that this responsibility entails proper, clear experiences and environment for the child to be raised, and that the child successfully completes all *stages of development*. It further states that the parents must, through example, empower the child with experiences that will allow the child to make responsible, wise decisions once the child turns into an adolescent and leaves the care of the parents. This age in a balanced world would be fifteen. However, in this imbalanced world it is twenty-two. Because parents, in most cases, are not able to comply with this universal law, we have a very disturbed world where many children remain psychologically and emotionally children into their thirties and even further. This fact deserves attention and a solution.

The solution is simple. Parents need to pay attention to their responsibility to evolve, so they may pass on clear understanding about how to live to their children. Children's responsibility is to ask questions and learn how to be a human from their parents. Parents need to be patient and responsive to their children's responsibility. Are you patient with yourself? Learn to be. Then you may be patient with others.

There is much to be taught about how to successfully raise a child, and I cover this more in the book *Empower Our Children.*

Passing the responsibility a biological parent has on to another person is not an option. A biological parent must always be responsible for the life the parent creates. Let me elaborate more. As a parent, you may give your child to a caretaker to raise: a stepfather or stepmother, grandfather and grandmother, or even an adoption agency. Still, know that you are responsible, even though you pass the care of the child on to another. For instance, if two parents decide to separate, the parent the child goes with must stay in contact with the other parent so the responsibility can be upheld. There are exceptions to this law, in the case of a parent breaking universal laws pertaining to the child's physical, emotional, mental and spiritual balance. This is a fine line and needs to be looked at carefully. Under the same law, if one parent is clearly inhibiting the child's ability to develop, then the other parent must take action appropriately and proportionally as the situation requires. This is a generalization compared to the great understanding required to create and successfully raise a child.

Pregnancy, carrying and delivering a child is sacred and deserves attention. The child, of course, is built from the mother and though there is a filter, of sorts, helping detoxify the blood and nutrients before reaching the fetus, it does not filter everything, especially heavy toxicity.

The body is a sacred vessel for your soul and the child's, and it must be *pure* in the conceiving and pregnancy processes.

- Your diet must be of the purest food and drink: absolutely no alcohol, tobacco, drugs or caffeine.

- Take into consideration everything you put into your body and breathe into your lungs. It will affect your child.

- Please refrain from exhaustion and overuse of the body.

The mind is another vital aspect of the child's development. All of your thoughts are creating and will affect the consciousness of the baby.

- Do your best not to stress or overwork the mind.

- Keep loving, peaceful thoughts about you.

- Remain clear in emotions as well. It all adds up when creating life.

- The male must respect this special time of the female, and during pregnancy strive to make it the best experience for the mother as possible.

Then, you will know you did your best for the soul that is coming into your child. Congratulate yourself and celebrate life!

ABORTION

It is the truth when I speak of your choice regarding the life that you have created. A sincere decision must be made at the point of conception to keep the baby. It is required for the soul to have a smooth entry into the body. If even by the grace of God, you are unable to decide on keeping the child's life, then you may abort the baby. When a child comes into the world without the confidence and commitment of the parents it will suffer greatly. If you do not commit to your baby, then you may abort it. This violates the natural laws of procreation. However, in this time you must not bring forth more children incapacitated with the ability to lead their lives. If you do not choose the life of the child, there will be an imbalance created; even so, it would be a greater imbalance if you created and bore life without a commitment to it. I apologize for this rather harsh understanding, for it is hard for any mother to make this type of a decision. In the future it will become more common to keep the child as this world clears its perspective. Until then, you may abort the life that you create.

In this time of the world, you will find accidents regarding conception. If your child is an accident and you do not want the child, you may abort it. At this time there are more unwanted children than there are miracles in this world. I have a strong opinion about the way you bring life into this world. If it is not intentional, or at least celebrated once you find out about the conception, you may abort it.

Let us revive the true nature of procreation and bring this world to a new understanding, one that embraces life and the challenge life brings, one that creates out of love rather than fear and a sense of duty.

In life there is choice and there is challenge. Without *choice*, you have no *challenge*. In the interim of the changing philosophy of sex and procreation, please be as responsible as you can for your actions and thoughts.

You will become clear. I believe in you.

There still remains the fact that we are in a transition, and because of this transition there will be universal laws that are broken. There are circumstances that at this time require abortion, whereas in a few years that may change. To circumvent the great opposition to natural laws, this world must take drastic action, one of which is to eliminate the inability for a human to live properly. This requires certain flexibility with the experience of abortion. Understand that during this interim period, abortion is allowed under certain circumstances. Soon when the world evolves, you will not need abortion. Creating life is a natural, sacred process and soon the world will understand.

ENERGETIC SEXUAL IMPRINTS

Every human indeed was designed to procreate. It is as natural as sleeping or breathing. It is a very pleasurable experience to inspire people to create new life. There is a common thought about creating life that is not clear. Humans feel they can have as much sex as they want and that there are no consequences. Sex is for one reason only, to procreate. If you have sex without the intention, primarily, of procreation, then you are not following the natural laws of procreation. There can be very serious consequences including death by disease and unsafe situations surrounding sex.

The most common consequence among all who break the laws of procreation is *energetic imprints* left from the intimate sharing during sex. You connect physically with your partner during sex, and you also connect energetically, such as the feeling you may get when your partner is thinking about you from a distance. The imprint left by the person you have sex with will *always* be with you, and it is a *deep* imprint. When you converse with someone an imprint is left, though the imprint left during sex can create the deepest imprint of any exchange between two humans. This is one reason sexual assault is so traumatizing as opposed to verbal assault.

You must be certain of your partner's energy before you have sex, for an imbalance in them may be detrimental to you. Be very certain of your partner's vibration of energy emotionally, physically, mentally and spiritually. Again, make sure you are compatible *energetically* with your partner. This must be emphasized, for it has a huge impact on people.

PLANNING TO PROCREATE

When deciding to procreate, clarity must be made. Parents often base the acceptance of procreating on the physical sustenance that they may provide for the child. Understand that the physical sustenance is only a part of the entire picture. It is important to be able to physically provide food, shelter and a healthy environment for your child. Take into consideration what many do not:

- How are you mentally and emotionally with the idea of procreating?

- Is there constant imbalance within you that will take your attention away from what your child needs?

- Do you need to clear yourself before you procreate?

Every parent-to-be should take into consideration the true wants and desires they have and how that will compete with the child.

- To what degree are you willing to sacrifice your wants and desires for the child's wellbeing?

These are serious questions to be asked. In reference to the above paragraphs, procreation is to be planned or if a conception is not planned, at least do as much planning and deciding at the earliest stages of pregnancy. Willingly, each parent must consider group or family counseling to decide if the parents can and want to live together and raise the child. If they do not decide to be together, they most likely will not procreate with each other.

It is human nature to want to be a part of the child's life and to be involved in raising and providing for the child. If a parent is imbalanced in any way, it will directly affect their ability to confidently raise the child with all necessary experiences for the child's development. The world is obviously imbalanced, and you, as a parent, may contribute to the greater evolution of Earth by carefully considering your reality before procreating. You owe this to yourself, and under the law of oneness, you would want this for the child and the world.

Most of what you have experienced with raising a child from the point of conception to adolescence is tainted by an unclear perspective on what a child needs to successfully develop. In the chapters to come, this will be lightly touched upon, though at some point there may need to be volumes of books dedicated to the natural raising of children.

Children are your number one asset in the evolution of your soul and a better world. If your soul does come to Earth again, it will be your actions and decisions on raising your children that will directly affect the next life you come to live.

- There is no escaping the damage you have done here on Earth, so would you please take responsibility and change this world?

When you look back on your life, you will look at the great things you could have done, or you will celebrate the great things you did do. It is truly your choice.

Allow your mind to let go for a moment of everything you have previously thought about abortion and sex, and also allow yourself to love whatever is presented to you in life. If you by the very grace of God become pregnant, then look at it as a *gift* and retain a balanced consciousness through the entire experience of pregnancy and raising the child.

A *clear perspective* is the understanding that the child's development is solely based on your love for the child.

- Your child will know if you aren't clearly showing love.

- The child knows what is in your heart and mind.

- You may think otherwise and hide things from your child, but your child knows you.

A lower-class status family may barely be putting food on the table, yet have the greatest love, and the child will successfully develop. An upper-class family may provide all the toys and things, yet have imbalanced love, and the child may not successfully develop.

It is love that is eternal and it is love that evolves.

Chapter 12

THE EXCHANGE AND KUNDALINI

There is an evolved understanding of lovemaking. It is not a physical experience, per say, but rather an energetic, nonphysical experience.

Have you ever been strongly drawn to someone, almost as if there was a cord attached to the two of you, and you could feel the feelings vibrating in your body?

This is called *Free Form Energy Exchange*, and it is done on evolved worlds in the place of what lovemaking is to you. The words *lovemaking* and *sex* have been used interchangeably by this world to mean the same thing: physical sexual intercourse. Since sex is only to be used for procreation, I am giving you a replacement that is more fulfilling on many levels.

In Free Form Energy Exchange, which I will refer to as *The Exchange*, you are connecting with one or more human beings energetically, giving you the elation similar to an orgasm. This orgasm that you receive is not physical, though you feel it very physically. The orgasm is also not confined to the sexual area of the body, but instead to every chakra of the body, giving orgasmic experiences throughout the entire body, if performed accurately. I will speak in detail about this because of the importance of a sex alternative.

First, it's important to understand the mechanism behind this exchange. It is at a *soul level*, you might say. It is when a facet of Divinity may directly connect with another facet of Divinity while in physical life. It is remarkable, and what many mystics strive for on this world.

One could live their entire life celibate and be far more pleasured with The Exchange instead of sex. One does not need the act of sex. One does, however, benefit greatly from The Exchange. This great accomplishment allows your soul to interact more directly with another soul through the physical. It is a huge achievement to attain this type of service to your soul.

Understand the energies behind sex. You invoke mental, emotional, psychic and spiritual energies. Also, you invoke physical energies known as *chi* and *kundalini*. To add to this, you experience a physical sensation of penetration. The combination of all these qualities of sex makes for a very powerful experience. Everyone taps into the energies in different ways, and this gives you a unique experience of sex. Your own evolution with these qualities will determine the strength of the qualities felt.

For example, some have strong mental fields and so the act of sex is particularly mental. Emotional personalities will experience sex emotionally. Physical beings will experience the feeling of penetration more strongly. It's amazing, the uniqueness of each sexual experience.

- The Exchange is only attained by a clear person, and to the degree your energies are clear, you will accomplish The Exchange.

- It is not sexual. It is an intimate love exchange that happens through the body and personality of a person.

- You may be any age or type of person.

- The Exchange is primarily based on the soul, not on the physical.

- It is the true essence and pure expression of intimacy.

- It may be done with parent and child or mother and father.

- It may be done with friends or any combination of relationship types.

- It is an energetic exchange not bound by distance.

- You could have The Exchange over the phone with someone, or schedule a time and have it with them without direct voice or physical contact.

- Because it is energetically based, there are few limitations. Time is a limitation because of the real time nature of The Exchange.

- If you are doing it with someone other than your actual sexual partner, absolutely clear your mind of any connection between sex and The Exchange.

If, with your thoughts, you connect The Exchange with sex and perform it with someone outside your sexual relationship, it will draw an experience of sex with that person. It is not sex. Please do not associate sex with it. Instead, it is a sex alternative and has a much greater use than sex.

It is not likely that everyone will be able to do The Exchange immediately. All of your chakras must be open and that requires clearing to be done in many instances. One use of sex is to move your chi, which is a universal energy that connects and supplies sustenance to all life. A form of chi is kundalini, which is meant to circulate in your energy *all the time*. Many have thought this only happens in a highly evolved person, and yes it does, but there are tools that you can use to move your kundalini.

There is fear about opening the kundalini because of the power of it. If your chakras are closed down and you force your kundalini to move, you could experience some discomfort, most commonly being ungrounded. It is not recommended to do exercises to force anything in your body, but rather ones that encourage and evolve you at a balanced pace. If you force anything, you are really going against the law of self-love and will feel consequences.

The reason it is essential to have your kundalini moving properly is that it is required for The Exchange. Many have misconceptions about the kundalini. One is that for it to be moving, you will feel physically a strong energy pulsing through your body, particularly along the spine. It is possible, though this is not necessary. You may feel kundalini moving on a more subtle level as well, and sometimes a person will not feel it moving at all. It is a life-sustaining energy that is needed for proper evolution into an adult.

When you are born, kundalini is moving properly. It isn't until you start closing your chakras down, by fears taken on from the world, that it slows down or stops completely.

When the kundalini stops, your body starts deteriorating. Even at a young age children can create health imbalance by blocking their kundalini. It is sustenance for not only the body but also the mind, emotions and other energies. It is very important to work on clearing the blocks that inhibit your kundalini.

Physical exercise such as aerobics and cardiovascular are more intense approaches, while yoga, tai chi and other simple movements are less intense approaches that will open the chakras and move the chi and kundalini. These energies are essential. Every person living can benefit from doing exercise every day.

One attachment of sex is that it does move the kundalini and opens the chakras in most people, thereby creating a great feeling on many levels. The person then associates the wellbeing with sex and not the kundalini being moved. When your kundalini is moving you have an overall sense of wellbeing and joy. Things can seem just right.

1. Understanding where your kundalini energy is blocked will give you some guidance into your problems.

2. Then, you will use The Five Accomplishments to clear the blocks.

Here is some general guidance that is not to be adhered to in every instance:

- The kundalini moves from the first chakra, just below the base of the spine.

- You must be grounded for it to move.

- It will move up the back as far as there are no energetic blocks, and then continue to circulate over the head and back down in front of you, creating an oval circle within your greater total energy.

- As it moves up and over it activates other energies and chakras. This may give you different sensations.

- You may experience heightened feelings, centeredness, love, acceptance, peace, the ability to speak your truth, visions, verbal messages, healing, wisdom and a myriad of others.

The following are some examples of imbalances related to the seven main chakras.

CHAKRA IMBALANCES

1. FIRST CHAKRA

   If the kundalini is blocked at the first chakra, you may be ungrounded or physically unhealthy.

2. SECOND CHAKRA

   The second chakra may be blocked due to imbalance in the stages of development of the personality.

   It could also signify an imbalanced perspective on procreation and sex in general.

It is a great indicator that you are not paying attention to your connectedness with your body. In this case you would *nurture* yourself.

3. THIRD CHAKRA

If you are not accepting your emotions and feelings completely, which most do not, then you may have a blocked third chakra.

It is also important to find beliefs associated with taking on another's experience. This is usually done at the third chakra.

The final aspect of this chakra is to *love* the source of where the feelings and emotions are coming from. Many do not accept themselves because they don't want to accept that such emotions would come from them.

4. FOURTH CHAKRA

Acceptance of yourself on a larger level correlating with thoughts and your greater experience has to do, generally, with the heart or fourth chakra. You might say this is the chakra of accepting your experience entirely and not placing pressure on yourself, which is usually felt physically on this area of the body. This means to clear any regret or attachments to an expectation of an outcome.

Eventually by clearing this chakra completely, you will experience pure love for yourself and for the God in all of Creation, under the law of oneness.

5. FIFTH CHAKRA

Your fifth chakra is directly related to speech and truth. You may accept your truth, but if the fifth chakra is blocked, you may have a fear of what others are going to think about you and your truth. To balance the fear, you will realize that it is the unique differences in each other that the world grows from, and by *sharing* your truth you evolve and serve the world in the greatest ways.

It is also associated with premature, imbalanced speech, as with those who always have to say something. They may speak a thought or emotion prematurely without discerning, at all, how to speak it or in what timely manner. These types of people, in some cases, do not acknowledge the truth others may have to share and take over conversations. These people have been known as know-it-alls, and can have an imbalance in the throat as well.

6. SIXTH CHAKRA

The sixth chakra blocked will mean several things. Most commonly is the way in which the person has learned to see the world. If it is blocked, there is some aspect of themselves or the world that they are not choosing to see. This may cause headaches, particularly, and pressure around the head.

This chakra is not as imperative, as far as correlating to your overall experience. However, it can cause a real resistance to the kundalini as it moves up.

7. SEVENTH CHAKRA

The seventh chakra is part of a soul awareness. So you might say it has a grander perspective. If you have trouble seeing the larger picture in situations or do not feel very wise, this chakra may be blocked. It has to do with putting the pieces of your life together and seeing a greater wisdom.

It is blocked in people who do not believe in a power greater than themselves such as a *creator* or *soul*. If one is in denial of their *higher self*, they will lack a greater wisdom that can make sense of any situation and lead them through any challenge. The seventh chakra is the connection to clear nonphysical communication and the realization of a person's *greater self*.

When this chakra is open, a person will know their purpose and seek to fulfill their destiny.

An overly analytical mind may block the seventh chakra by needing to make sense of the seemingly nonlinear experiences through it.

> This chakra will be like a compass leading someone to their highest potential and destiny. If blocked, the person will struggle in life.

Open up to the vast abundance and horizons available to you as a clear being. One reason that you will choose to clear your experiences is to move the kundalini, though there are many reasons to do so.

There are many uses for kundalini energy but number one is physical wellbeing. Kundalini is necessary for your choice of not aging, because it is the life sustenance energy that rejuvenates and replenishes your body.

How do you know, particularly, when your kundalini is moving?

There are several significant factors when kundalini moves:

- You have energy and need less sleep in most cases.
- Your mind is clearer and emotions are more easily accessible.
- Everything in your life seems to be accentuated, and your intuition opens up as a result of it.
- There can be a physical sensation that rolls up the spine and circulates. This sensation may be as simple as a sense, to a strong pulse vibrating, or a tingling that makes your hair stand up on end.

Interesting points regarding The Exchange:

- The energy will take you into a slightly altered space of awareness. For the time you engage in it, you will be in a timeless and sometimes weightless feeling that can last as long as you decide.

- You will invoke this energy by the openness you intend to have with your partner. It must be mutual. One or the other may block The Exchange.

There are many benefits of The Exchange. Some include:

- You may have access to your soul on a clearer level.

- You will know the person you share it with in ways you hadn't before.

It is completely up to the individual how to experience it:

- It could be as simple as lying next to a loved one and feeling The Exchange subtly as a field of energy around you. This is the most basic experience of it, being a general overall exchange.

- A clearer and more focused experience of The Exchange would be for you and the other person to intentionally open up to one another completely, and allow your main chakras to exchange energy.

You do want to make sure the person you are doing The Exchange with is energetically compatible. You probably won't choose to do it with just anyone.

It is done to commune on a soul-to-soul level with a physical sensation benefit. The point though, is the communion among souls, and the physical sensations are an added bonus that can really create a demand for this exchange.

This will be the intercourse of the next one thousand years. More and more people will be clear enough to experience it. There will be classes and videos teaching it, just like there are tantra or yoga videos and classes. Once this form of exchange is accepted, the world will significantly turn around.

Thank you for your consideration with such a drastic change in lifestyle. It is a wonderful validation of the soul to receive an exchange of this magnitude.

THE EXCHANGE TECHNIQUE

Eventually you may do The Exchange spontaneously and at a distance. In the meantime, this thirteen-step exercise will help you in the beginning stages.

1. To participate in the exchange, you will probably want to *prepare* ahead of time. This is to bring balance to your energy and allow you to connect on a deeper level.

2. Start by using the concepts previously discussed such as regular *exercise* for fifteen days. The more you move your body, the better.

3. Then, lie next to your partner for The Exchange, and notice how your energy *feels* different to lie next to them.

4. Get as *close* as you can to them without actually touching them, and notice how your energy *feels*.

5. Talk about your experience. The *openness* and *sharing* you have with your partner will directly affect the results.

6. It is important to *clear your mind.* This experience is not of the mind at all. It is again, of the soul, and the soul expresses itself on a *feeling level* which is different than your typical emotions.

   The *feeling of the soul* is pure love and compassion. You will feel this greater when lying close to your partner with an openness. To the degree you are open will affect the intensity of the feeling.

7. Close your eyes and *imagine you are one* with your partner in every way. One with them emotionally, physically, mentally and spiritually. *Visualize merging* with them and *feel* this.

8. Watch how you speak because abrupt speech can shake the connection. Sometimes there are no words needed,

and if you *speak*, do so as *gently* as possible without affecting the flow of your experience.

If you are having difficulty with the first part (steps one through eight) of The Exchange, you may spend as much time as you need with it before moving on to the second part (steps nine through thirteen). Use the *Chakra Clearing Meditation* and *Chakra Opening Exercises*, described later in this book, to help you remove blocks and open up your chakras.

9. FOURTH CHAKRA OPENING

First, open the fourth chakra and connect at a heart level. When you connect your heart chakra with your partner's, you will feel a *stirring sensation* in that area of your body, particularly, and when you do, you know The Exchange is happening as it should.

Remember to focus on the *feelings*.

Let all thoughts go, and connect to the person's soul on a feeling level through these physical insertion points called chakras.

10. THIRD CHAKRA OPENING

Next, connect your third chakra. This is the feeling center of the body and it is the largest chakra, so you most likely will feel this one stronger. Allow it to swirl and stir and finally flow between you and your partner.

11. SECOND CHAKRA OPENING

Then, connect at the second chakra in the area below the belly button around the reproductive organs. Let this stir and swirl and then move between you and your partner.

12. SIXTH CHAKRA OPENING

Finally, the sixth chakra will open between you and your partner. You may feel pressure or tingling. When this opens, you will see on an inner level, the feelings you are sharing with your partner's soul. You will see the soul with your feelings. It will probably be unlike anything else you have experienced.

13. COMPLETE CHAKRA OPENING

Once these four primary chakras are exchanging energy, the rest of your chakras will automatically begin the energy exchange.

You can look forward to anything happening:

- You may be *healed* or reveal *past lives* with the person.
- You could have remembrance of your *existence without a body* in the Nonphysical Realm.
- You may *understand* things on a deeper soul level.

- And most of all, you will *commune* as a soul.

You are a soul, and in this exchange you can completely immerse yourself in your soul and its communion with another soul.

Probably you will not experience anything in life grander than a clear energy exchange. Good luck!

CHAKRA OPENING EXERCISES

CHAKRA OPENING VISUALIZATION EXERCISE

1. If you get stuck, you can imagine or visualize the chakra you're having trouble with opening and sharing energy.

CHAKRA OPENING HAND EXERCISE

1. Another technique is to simply take your open palm hand, and open the chakra by spinning your hand about two inches away from your body in a circular, clockwise motion as if the clock is on your body.

2. You would go from your right side, up and over to the left side, and then down and back around to the right side, with your hand over the chakra.

Know these are tools, and do not form a dependency on them. Eventually you want to find the root of your blocks and be clear and free from everything.

One aspect of The Exchange, that is exciting, is your participation with God. I will describe this in detail in a later book. It involves creating miracles with this exchange. Because you are invoking a soul-level experience, you have the ability to manifest God's presence, with intention and direction.

It is true that *group consciousness* can be more powerful than *individual consciousness*. If you have one or more partners participating with you in The Exchange, you can literally move hills and levitate objects. You have God's power, or at least in most cases near God's power, at your disposal. It is a phenomenal step to sovereign absolute power. You may use partners to formulate your creative power and eventually manifest the above abilities alone.

This advanced teaching is used on evolved worlds for anything from building structures and healing nature, to levitating objects, to manifesting food and water out of thin air.

The power of creation begins with this exchange.

Witness it this century.

Chapter 13

NEW GENERATIONS OF CHILDREN

There are numerous people speaking about a time when we must stand and confront the inadequacies of this world. You know them well. Even children are aware of the discomfort they feel in the world.

Children are the hope and you must understand something about them. Since 1969 children have been different. Their souls came in more evolved. Some are older souls. Others are altogether different.

Many believe there are aliens on this planet and there are, but not as you probably think. What is an alien? The truth is that an alien is a soul who has lived on a planet other than Earth. When you think of it this way, it is not so alien to you.

There are thousands of planets that have intelligent life, or in other words life forms that house souls. Beyond that, there are millions that require more evolution to sustain a suitable life form for a soul to live in.

You have theories that they come in space ships and land on your planet to secretly live amongst you. This phenomenon is rare, though it does occur frequently on other planets. Physical aliens who do travel in spaceships to Earth acknowledge your development and will not interfere until you, as a collective people on Earth, consciously decide you will embrace their existence and interaction with Earth. You have a way to go before you will evolve to this point. You still see them as a threat and not an ally.

The reality is that souls from other planets have been born on Earth in great numbers since the 1960's. These children are different than you in many ways. Most of these souls are from planets more evolved than Earth, so it is hard for them, at first, to adjust to the imbalance of Earth. The unclear perspective of love is new to them, and in many cases they turn to drugs or other devices to escape this world's reality.

The point is that there are increasingly different children among you, and you must respect them for what they have chosen to do. They chose to leave the nature of their world to participate with Earth for this Age of the Soul. In doing so, their intention is to elevate your world's consciousness.

There is a great celebration in the cosmos with what is happening right now. The important consideration is that you have an abundance of help to evolve and create a different world for yourselves.

- Will you *resist* the change, or will you *embrace* it?

Please decide now, because if you put it on a shelf for later, there most likely will be no later. Humans have a great capacity for procrastination.

The new generations of children have been called many things by the people of Earth. I respect the authority of those who have attempted to categorize these children; however, there is to be no categorization. Believe me when I say, you only have a small perspective of the larger picture with these children, and an attempt to categorize them and make them feel more different than they already feel is disappointing at best. They must not be categorized but simply looked at with a *new perspective*.

Look at the new generations of children with the intention of embracing love and learning with them how to live clearly. These children came to journey your trials with you. They are doing it whether you know it or not. So be open to their purpose, and learn with them how this world will change and survive its inadequacies. The children are your hope for a better world the next time you choose to live another life. They, again, are your greatest asset for a new beginning. Journey the new beginning with them and help them understand how this world can change.

You, as a parent, must respect that you are an authority figure and will still set the rules for your child. The difference is to listen to them, and adjust your rules according to how it can benefit your old understanding and the new understanding that you receive in this book.

Listen To Your Child.

Flexibility is vital in new ways of perceiving the raising and disciplining of your child.

In the end, it is the best that you can do that will stand out as an accomplishment, so please do your best and do not regret your decisions as a parent or teacher.

The children know you, in many cases, better than you know yourself because of their increased intuition, which I will speak more about later. The veil that was drawn at birth for the children, dividing the Physical and Nonphysical Universes, is thinner than your veil. Every generation of children will have a thinner and thinner veil. The point will come when the Nonphysical and Physical Universes will coexist together, as they already do, though it will be noticeable and understandable. Therefore, most of the children, if developed properly, will have a phenomenal intuition and sense about things.

There is much to be learned about the new generations of children. First and foremost is the education system regarding the kids. Orchestrate a new education system immediately. It will take great determination to do so. The way you teach and the way you expect the kids to learn is not working. You have many imbalances, or as you would say *flaws*, in the current education systems, and it requires attention urgently.

Your education systems are not providing adequate support for the proper development of children, which is violating universal laws. One who takes on the responsibility of a child in the absence of the parents, as a school and teacher do, is required to provide a balanced environment and system for the child to successfully complete the stages of development. This is not happening with most education systems. This means you need to change them.

This will require an entire overhaul of the way you approach education. Your world, for the most part, puts more value on economic and technological growth than the well-being of your children. What is this saying? You will reap serious consequences if you do not change now. Let me explain.

You are force-feeding the new generations of children serious drugs so you don't have to change anything. It doesn't stop there.

You are depriving children of the nourishment they need most—*love*. This word has been misconstrued for thousands of years. When it is needed most, you are distancing your children from it the most. You do this by determining that it is the child who has the problem and not the adult or caretaker. You absolutely need to *rethink* this mounting situation.

Parents are listening to doctors, who have little understanding of what the child is actually going through, and ignoring the child.

Then as a parent, you force the child to take drugs. The only difference between what you give them and street drugs is the purity. Pharmaceutical drugs are pure chemicals and street drugs are typically not pure chemicals.

Then you, as a society, wonder why drug dependency has increased at astronomical rates. This very atrocity is a significant benefit for the drug and medical industry because they profit from the entire process, which encompasses rehab, overdoses, surgery, and the psychological, emotional and physical imbalances created. The government is excited on a subconscious level because all of this keeps people in a numb, sleepy state where they can be easily maneuvered. This is no conspiracy. This is fact.

You may take this information for what you feel is truth and leave the rest for later, but please at least consider this. You have a responsible role to fill in this world, even if you do not have children. Under the law of self-love you must look at what's happening and the repercussions it has on your future lifetimes.

Do research and look into this, though it is very self-explanatory:

1. Parents don't understand kids.

2. Parents listen to other parents or doctors.

3. Parents make kids take drugs.

4. Parents don't know it, but they are creating drug dependency.

5. Many drug dependant kids grow up into drug dependant adults.

6. Drug dependant adults need help with their dependency.

7. Financially, drug companies, medical professionals and the government benefit from the entire length of this epidemic.

It is very easy to understand and it is in plain sight, especially in America.

➢ What is a solution you can participate in right now?

You don't have to fight any of this. The government, drug companies and medical industry are not entities you need to fight. If you do not give something energy, it goes away. Simply *change your focus* away from these unbalanced solutions and onto something else. The natural solutions from a pure love perspective may be more challenging for you, and may take a little more time. However, what you are doing is setting up a *long-term solution* rather than a choice that will open up a greater imbalance. The kids need you now more than ever.

As time goes on, you will see greater and greater imbalances as a result of your choices to ignore the problem or cover it up with what seems to be immediate resolve. The truth is that, for the most part, the professionals don't know any more than you do about the clear reality behind all of this. In most cases, you know much more than the professionals.

What makes a professional? Many consider a professional one who has an educational background. In medicine the education is to treat humans by cutting, burning or drugging. Many alternatives outside of these solutions are against the medical professions' laws, and might result in a termination of employment and licensure to practice medicine. This is what is happening.

You, as a people, have been conditioned to take a pill if you sense an imbalance in your body, or to go to a psychotherapist if you have an imbalance in your emotions or mind. How many professionals actually empower you with cures, rather than bandages to cover the symptoms? The symptoms, as explained earlier in the book, are often not the root, but rather the indicators. If you camouflage your indicators they will not go away. This is why, in most cases, you are required to be on drugs your entire life or see a psychotherapist for years. It doesn't take years to get to the root of a symptom. It can take minutes or seconds. What takes you twenty years with a psychotherapist can take a few minutes or hours to transform with The Five Accomplishments. There are other ways than what has been known. Share these new ways with the world. Help this world grow and live free from the bondage of your ancestors. Give your children a new start.

Does one empower you to be independent of them or their system of thought, or do they attach you into their experience by saying, in some form or another, that you *need* them? This is a great indicator of truth.

Yes, humans are interdependent such as with the automobile manufacturer that creates an automobile for you to drive to where you need to go, or the market that provides produce for you to eat. You could be independent of these things, though they make your life easier.

Philosophically you feel on some level that the approach of drugs and other tools to live by are needed, and they are not. You have been conditioned, since birth, to rely on the government and entities outside of you to make choices for you. You have allowed them to tell you what is best for you, and you have followed. It is time to make your own mind up on your life. It is time to change the system. It starts with you.

An organization only has power over those who give it power. Empower yourself with *choice* and *discernment* of what is best for you. Use this book to empower you with a *direct connection* to all of your answers and needs. You have been disconnected from your power for so long that it seems unreal to think you have all the power in your hands to create anything you need. Doesn't it?

- Do you honestly feel from all of the conditioning of your life that you can create anything for yourself? Isn't this a concept only heard about?

- You must ask yourself, "Do I want to be powerful?"

I must say, yes you do. Every being at some level wants to be powerful.

Get in touch with it.

Feel it . . . See it . . . Know it . . . Hear it . . . Be it.

Decide you will own your sovereign power as a soul.

AFFIRMATION OF EMPOWERMENT

Affirm:

> "I will not put my power outside of myself.
>
> I am *all-powerful*. I am *connected* to God *directly*.
>
> I will find my answers and fulfill my needs by my direct connection to God.

I am truly ready to move forward and I will co-create a better world. It starts with me today.

Thank you God for this opportunity.

I am blessed to have you in my life all the time. You are always with me, and I give my will to you to show me a road I have not seen. I have faith in you to guide me through my challenges and to provide for my needs.

I Am A New Person."

Chapter 14

NEW WORLD UNIVERSITY

Part of the renewed world will be changing the perspective of adults, or rather young adults. This will happen through the construction of a University.

I am impressing upon many people, intuitively, the dire need for an education overhaul.

1. We will start with a University.

2. Then, build a smaller school for kindergarten through twelfth grade.

3. Later, after the University has been established for a while, the addition of a hospital will be necessary to expand the overview of the larger plan.

The University will be similar in many ways to traditional schools in that there will be a curriculum necessary for achieving any doctorate, masters or bachelors degree that we offer. Also, for licensure and certification for professions such as a medical doctor (M.D.) and marriage family therapist (M.F.T.), there will be all required coursework offered to successfully prepare and transition students into the accepted mainstream. Upon completion of the coursework, students will have all the necessary tools to move forward in their chosen professions. The University will be fully accredited as any other well-established, respected university.

The intention behind the construction of this University is to work *within* the system, and transform it from the inside out. Many have sought to fight the system. This is a way, and usually is not beneficial to the one fighting or the one being fought.

Professionals interested in making a difference in the way our world operates its education are frustrated by the necessity found to change the teaching and coursework. Once a teacher acknowledges this necessity and makes the desired changes or presents them to a supervisor, they find disappointment in the unwillingness to change long-term patterns of practice that, in the eyes of the oversight of a university, is not practical. This is why this University will be built upon universal laws and the openness of a new way to teach, learn and operate, even the minute details of the school.

By working within the accepted system, the University will have a different approach as seen from the outside, but from the inside the school will literally be alive. What is meant by alive? There is a living essence, you could call a spirit of sorts, but really it is a nonphysical committee that will be in direct relation with the board of directors of the school. Both the nonphysical and physical board of directors will operate on an equal level, and in direct communication with one another. This will require each board member to understand and be able to channel and communicate intuitively with the nonphysical beings. Of course, this is not a normal practice, though to put God in control is necessary.

What you will actually find is that every government body, family and group that has any kind of integral role on an individual, group or global level, will embrace the relationship with nonphysical beings and the advice they have. It will be a true working relationship, considering they do have a greater perspective than humans do.

The *living essence* of the University is already in existence. Now it is a matter of tapping into it and manifesting it into the physical so you can experience it. For a school to be run and operated from this living essence is a new idea, and is exactly the type of operating procedures for business, family and government that will be implemented in the new world. God is expecting to live amongst you unlike ever before, and it starts with your openness and consideration that such a thing is possible.

The professionals that graduate from this University will have a solid understanding of what the world expects from them, given their credentials, and something much more—an open intuition they are able to effectively use in their profession.

Every walk of life can benefit from the natural God-given *intuitive inner senses*. The intuitive inner feeling, hearing, knowing and seeing senses were created by God. Your spoken language was created by humans. The difference is clarity and impact.

Understand and use your intuitive senses. They are mandatory for seeing the world clearly. By doing so, you may navigate through your profession unlike you ever could without them.

For instance, imagine:

- A medical doctor, who is seeing someone for back surgery, and can intuitively understand that the person doesn't need surgery at all. What they really need is a natural remedy that will save them the cutting of their body and the cost of surgery.

- The business professional will intuitively know the company's best interest every time.

- The inventor will receive knowledge about new technology intuitively.

- Businesses will intuitively know the best way to implement the inventions.

This is why it is so imperative to cultivate and nurture the intuitive inner senses. By doing so, everyone can work together for the greatest good of all, through a direct connection to knowledge, wisdom and healing.

Another aspect that you will not see at other universities is the approach of teaching and learning. Students, teachers and all staff, for that matter, will be on an equal level. Under many universal laws concerning the self, groups and interaction, many of the accepted guidelines and methodology for teaching and learning will change. One of these is the remembrance criteria needed for many degrees such as the medical doctor.

There will be new technology for learning and fact cramming that will completely revolutionize the way students learn. The University will still provide the necessary knowledge that a student needs to graduate, but the method of learning will be something like hypnosis. The student will be encouraged to make the most use of their time by using video, audio and other tools to remember the seemingly endless knowledge for their profession. This technology of learning facts will free up the student to spend quality time on the greater pursuits of the University, like learning universal laws and how they apply in their profession.

Intuition and its usage in the student's chosen profession will be a consistent experience through the entire length of a major.

There is much to look forward to in this revolutionary way of experiencing truth through a school system. Truth is the key here and the truth will be told. In every way the truth will be upheld. Students will know everything about their profession, including the things that industries, governments and other schools want them to know, as well as the things they don't want them to know. As I have explained before, there is much behind the scenes in most industries and professions in the world. All facts will be revealed. Remember please that truth is truth. We as a school will not base the truth on outside opinion or profitability. Basing what you're willing to share upon what you get for it, in a basic sense, is prostitution. I will not have a school built upon prostitution. The truth will not be diluted. The truth can be told in an eloquent and nonbiased way to give an objective standpoint. Simply stated, here are the facts and it is your choice what to do with them. It is essential for every student to know the full scope of their major, and upon understanding it, decide if it is what they really want.

Every human attending the University will have a *guidance counselor*. This counselor will have a few more tools in the bag than your average counselor. The counselor will get to the *root* of what a student needs to succeed, not just in school, but in all areas of the student's life. This counselor will also provide the same services to the staff. Every human who is adding to the collective of the University will be gifted with weekly or biweekly counseling. It is important to look at the entire human to balance any area of the person's life. One of the most significant differences with the University's counselors is empowering the person with their soul's destiny. The counselors will share perspectives of how the direction a student or staff is choosing fits in with their soul's destiny, and how it can be adjusted. In essence, the experience of the University will be evolving every individual participating, on a soul level. The graduates will be of the wisest in their professions and in the world, because the new approach goes beyond physical data cramming, into the realm of infinite, eternal wisdom.

The creative aspect of the students will be stimulated to help them balance, what in most schools is, left-brain dominated or intellectual dominated curriculum. Most would say this is normal. However, it is not. The University will have the technology in place to help the students through this rather unfortunate requirement of the world's professions, in order to spend more time with the right-brain or creative curriculums.

With the proper balance in place, the University will become the most powerful in the world and will spread to every country. Eventually the new way of operating education will be embraced and practiced by the world, and at that point, every professional graduating from a university will be balanced and living from a completely different space than they are now. I look forward to celebrating this time ahead and encourage you to take immediate action.

I put a call out to every professional. Whether you are a cook or a director on a board, you are required to seriously look at the way you have participated with this world.

- Are you ready to make a significant difference in your life and the future lives of your soul?

This operation will need individuals from every walk of life, and there is room for everyone who feels this approach. I will honor every human who chooses to participate in this new design.

Please contact us through this book if you have an interest in this plan. It has already begun, and it is no coincidence that you are reading this book right now. Whether you are physically or energetically co-creating this University, you are welcome.

Thank you for your consideration in changing your life, and your willing openness to a completely new way of living. I bless you. You may call on me to help you decide, personally, your part in this greater picture. Know that the University is only the beginning. There is room for all and all are welcome.

Please know your worth and equality. You are loved. Be *kind* to yourself and *love* yourself as much as you possibly can.

Believe me when I say, you have come so far so fast. Look at your life—All the challenges and triumphs.

Bless You.

Chapter 15

HEALING AND SOUL-BASED LIVING

There is a completely new way of healing than has been previously practiced by the world. With few exceptions, there has been the perspective of a need to change someone to make them *better* or *perfect*, you might say. Please, let's get a very clear perspective on what making someone *better* is.

Who are you to say what someone needs? You don't even fully know what you need. Do you disagree? Would you say that every area of your life is in balance?

Please give me one good reason that you know better than another person knows.

Education is a likely answer. You are educated in a particular area.

- What determines that your education was a clear perspective?
- How do you know that a person needs to be changed?
- How do you know what they need to be changed to?

These are very important questions to ask yourself if you are taking on other's responsibilities.

- Why do you feel it is your duty to take on another's responsibilities?

Many would say, "Because I can." You can also jump out of an airplane without a parachute. Are you going to do that? What is the difference? The difference is *perspective*.

You are going to be challenged by this next section in the book, because most every person in the world is taking on other's responsibilities. This means most everyone is taking on my role, meaning God's role. Who are you to think you are in a place to judge what a person needs? Leave that up to me. I am all powerful, all knowledgeable, all present and timeless. There is none other than I that can be responsible for another. You must stop playing God and start playing your part. Your part is not to change anyone. Leave that up to the person to do.

If you think there is something out of balance in their perspective of life, you may offer your perspective. Though, if you do, please do it from an intention of *empowering* the person with their own answers, and not taking on the responsibility of providing all answers to them.

The mechanism of life is evolving through the challenge of *choice*. Humans must make choices and be responsible for their choices under universal laws. Humans have created their own universal laws and labeled them *wrong* and *right*, *good* and *bad*, and by doing this, humans have created a heavy burden and consequence under the law of cause and effect. You have played God for far too long. Please give people's power back to them and stop telling them what to do from a standpoint of absolute authority. Instead, create a new system of sharing perspectives and always honoring someone for the perspective they hold and choose to live. Then you are not responsible for their lives and the consequences thereof.

If you are a counselor for instance, and a client comes to you wanting a clear perspective in their relationship, it is your job to give them tools to empower them with a clear perspective. Instead of telling them what they *need* to do, give them options. For your information, a counselor, really of any kind, whether it is medical, psychological or other, is to give cause and effect perspectives. For instance, this is what is happening and what would you like to do about it? There must always be a choice with the client. There must always be the challenge of making the choice, or you are robbing your client of experiences and there will be consequences. How is this so? You, as a medical doctor or psychotherapist, are trained to diagnose and prescribe treatment. The patient or client is trained to listen and follow. There is little room for choice at all. You, as a professional, have a position of authority that is unclear. You have been taught to tell people what to do because you know what is *better* for them. Do you really?

- Why aren't all of your patients and clients cured?

Sure, there are intellectual facts and figures that can answer the last question.

- Are you going to be okay with the odds that only a percentage of those you treat are cured?

You have been trained that this is the way it is. I disagree. The truth is everyone can be cured, and there are simple, fast, proven ways to cure people of their imbalances.

1. First, make the decision you will accept everyone can be cured and there are methods to do so.

2. Then, you will be empowered to empower your clients.

- Do you even want your clients to be cured? That means no repeat business.

- Do you like the comfort of knowing a client will return again and again paying for your lifestyle, or is the clients best interest really first?

- If your patients are cured, the medical industry may pressure you and you may not be accepted by your colleagues. Is this okay with you, who are doctors and medical professionals?

Please *meditate* on these questions and comments. They will decide what your soul experiences the next time you live on Earth.

Once you decide how you want to exist, then you can make plans for your new goals and perspective.

Remember that what you choose is equally good. There is no judgment with your choices, only the balances your soul will create in-between your lives.

The reason there are so many imbalances in the world is that people have left the Source out of their lives for so long. You are raised to believe you need to do everything on your own. There is so much nonphysical assistance that few are aware of. The most significant tool you can give to someone is to show them how to directly communicate with the Source so they can receive their own answers. Then you, as a facilitator, will be a simple teacher to help empower them. If the client's best interest is really first, then you must *teach* them how to *empower* themselves.

Empowerment Is The Key To Evolution.

If you deprive one of their power, you are depriving them of evolution and unbalancing yourself under many laws.

It is imperative to stand for your truth and allow others to disagree. One imbalance of this world is raising children with the understanding that disagreement is not okay. People can disagree and still love one another, and it is important to give others a voice for their truth. The wars and crimes are primarily from disagreement being expressed in an imbalanced way.

Disagreement Is Just As Beneficial As Agreement.

Disagreement is what makes you unique from the next person. Interesting how the one quality that makes life worth living is not accepted. You are designed by God to be *unique* and have a *different perspective* than others. There is not one pair of people that agree on everything. It is impossible. You are like a snowflake. No two snowflakes are the same. They all hold their uniqueness. They are all special.

Under the laws of equality and self-love, people must be able to disagree in a constructive way. A constructive way is *love-based* rather than *fear-based.*

When a disagreement comes from love, it is for the love of self that you express it. You, in fact, state your truth because you love yourself enough to express yourself. You accept your thoughts and emotions and do not judge them, or in other words screen which thoughts and which emotions are okay to experience.

If you express disagreement from fear, it is rooted in the desire to change someone else. This can result in anger and even violence. When disagreement is expressed from fear, you are attempting to *control* the situation with either the words you use or the energy behind the words.

Please note that you may say nothing and the energy you are exuding with your thoughts is strong enough for the person to feel and respond to. The unspoken thought energy may be fear-based disagreement, and if it is, you will most likely get a response similar from the other person.

The reality behind thought energy is that what is unclear within you will *trigger* or *indicate* the same imbalance in another, and vice versa. It is very rare that a person is mostly clear. Therefore, and especially in relationships, two people trigger the similar imbalances in each other. Everything is vibrations and like will affect like. So if your partner does something that triggers anger in you, it is likely that what they did, you also have within you. This is a law of evolution called cause and effect. It is important that you really accept this law, because if you do, successfully, it can totally turn your world around from *blaming* to *understanding* and *learning*.

> As you come from *fear-based disagreement*, you will blame the other person with *judgment*.
>
> By coming from a *love-based disagreement*, you will attempt to *understand* the other person or experience by *learning*.

One is *reacting* and the other is *observing*.

You have a choice every moment to be the observer, which is love-based or *soul-based living*, or react and engage, which is fear-based or *ego-based living.*

You have a choice every moment of your life. You are giving your power away every time you react and engage in another person's story of life. Why would you choose to put your power outside of yourself? Become the *observer* and remain centered and aware.

When you react to an experience, you are being controlled. It is a very simple concept:

- Do you choose to be controlled or do you choose to be in control?

You are in control when you are not engaging.

Everyone has *stories* about life. It is up to you to choose your stories very wisely. Let go of stories that take you away from clear love using The Five Accomplishments. Embrace stories that bring you closer to clear love, and accept them as your truth. It is very simple.

- Every moment ask yourself, "Am I reacting and engaging or am I observing and learning?"

It is a choice. Becoming one with the experience of your soul is the great journey.

Please journey this with me now.

There are many aspects to the full experience of the soul for a human. It seems so distant to most that there are hardly any examples on Earth of a person living from the *soul perspective*. There are, however, many eager participants who desire, from the depths of their personalities, to become one with the perspective of the soul. It is possible, and you will accomplish it if you decide to.

➢ *Assert* your desire to be one with the perspective of your soul.

The beginning to the instructions is in this book, and I promise there will be more instruction. The coming books will not be as useful to you if you do not first commit and use this book to your fullest capability.

Part of the empowerment you will share with others is the tone you use as you teach and share your perspective on clear love. *Tone* can be interpreted as *energy* behind the words you speak. Tone expresses much more than the mundane words spoken. Be conscious of it.

Be conscious of the energy behind the words:

- What is your *intention*?
- Are you trying to control or change the person?
- What is your *perspective* relative to the person you are sharing with?

Every person is different, so there will be different approaches to every situation. There is not one cookie-cutter way to share a clear perspective with someone. It is essential to *respect* the uniqueness of an individual and be *patient* with their perspective. As you wish to be heard, so do they. Let it be from clear love.

More than you think, there are places and times you may express your love clearly. Please be conscious, at all times, if you are expressing the clearest love you are capable of.

1. Pay attention to responses you get from expressing love clearly, as opposed to unclearly. You will notice a difference.

2. Play with it. Talk about it with your loved ones and colleagues.

3. Remember you always have a choice of how to participate.

4. Determine you will evolve with every experience and every person you interact with, and with every one recalibrate your approach with clear love.

5. Finally, you will be an example of clear love for the world.

Until then, you may be an example of determination to become clear and that is a great virtue. You may, therefore, be an example every step of the way, and the world around you will benefit from your example. Thank you for your choice to lead through example. You are brave.

There are going to be those who will mock you for your bravery of leadership. They will speak against you because of your love for yourself and the evolution of the entire world. They will do this to mask emptiness within themselves. The world has learned to shame and blaspheme that which threatens the way they have always done things, especially entities that have an interest to keep things the same. There will always be this dilemma, until this world feels *safe with change*.

I am here to *comfort* you and help you feel safe with changing your life. No one will do this for you. It is completely up to you, and I am here to walk with you. I will *carry* you in situations where there is no way out for you. I will. I already am. Know me as the one you pray to and ask for guidance. Know me as the one who holds your head up when there is no one around. Know me as the one who will walk with you through this life until the end of time. I am and I will. Fear not. This life and world are transitory. They will pass by and you will live on. Your body and your life are not yours. They are used by you to get an experience. Once you are done with them, you will leave them behind and not look back. You will have no attachment to them. You may sacrifice your evolution by having attachments to your life and body, or you may liberate yourself by knowing they are of the Earth and the Earth is not your home. If you can release your fear of leaving your life and body, you can *live fearless*. Fear is a choice that is learned. It is a choice.

SOUL PATTERNS

The role of the *soul* is to observe and record experiences. It rarely interacts with your personality. When it does, your soul is careful not to interfere too much with your life.

On the other hand, the *personality* can become aware of and interact directly with the soul. Whether the soul returns the interest is up to the soul, not the personality. At some point, you clear yourself enough to become very aware of your soul, and may express the light or the essence of your soul through your personality.

> It is analogous to a *pure light*, representing your soul, shinning through a clear pane of glass, which represents your personality. This compared to a dirty or colored pane of glass will, by all means, give you a different experience. It is still the same soul energy or light, yet the experience of it is different depending on how dirty or colored your personality is. The point is to clear your personality so you may experience the pure light of your soul.
>
> Think of it also as a *light bulb*. You can cover the light bulb or color the light bulb, but the light source remains the same throughout.

It is important to be aware of the very clear distinction between a *soul pattern* and a *life pattern*. There is a huge difference.

- A *soul pattern* is the result of an experience the soul intends to receive, and is often carried across multiple lifetimes.

- A *life pattern* is not directly related to what the soul intends to receive, and is the result of life circumstances that shape the personality into experiencing specific behaviors and attitudes.

A soul pattern is usually exceptionally challenging to overcome and sometimes experienced for tens or hundreds of lifetimes. Soul patterns are not taken on by obligation, but rather from a choice the soul makes to gain certain experiences of physical living that add to its overall destiny.

There is a *list* of experiences your soul intends to receive during its physical lifetimes on Earth. These experiences could be interpreted as patterns because the soul will continue to create circumstances, lifetime after lifetime, until it completely receives what it has intended. Once the soul has completed all experiences on its list, it has graduated from the need to physically incarnate.

A soul remains the same throughout a lifetime, for the most part, but the personality created by the soul does change significantly throughout a lifetime, in fact it changes constantly.

Most of the soul's wisdom and evolution comes through evaluation in-between lifetimes. This crucial time is when the soul decides what experiences it will take on from its previous life and which ones it will not. This integration period is important to the soul's evolution; it is when a soul determines the next steps of its destiny based on its previous lifetime.

When the personality evolves during its life, the soul can have great moments called *initiations* that create pivotal points in the soul's evolution. The work is done through the accomplishments of the personality, not directly with the observing soul.

A soul healer or healing is not possible because it is the personality that changes during a lifetime, and it is the personality that a facilitator will directly work with, not the soul. A facilitator may possibly have intuitive communication with a soul, but this is not healing the soul, rather simply exchanging information with it.

One can, through extensive training, identify soul patterns:

1. By identifying the pattern a soul chose to experience in its physical lifetimes, one can then understand the most effective way to receive the lesson or growth opportunity from the pattern.

2. This may end or complete the pattern of the soul, depending on what the soul decides after its present lifetime.

This type of completion is magnificent and monumental in the destiny of the soul.

There are two reasons that your *personality* is not the same as your *soul*:

- Your *soul is pure love* without the emotional space that harbors fear, or the mental space that is limited by the human thoughts.

- Your soul needs a conduit between it and the Physical Universe, and this *conduit is the personality.* It can be no other way.

For a soul, who is your guide, to show itself physically to you would require it to take on a personality conduit, thereby lowering its vibration, in order to communicate and relate with you in the Physical Universe. You would be experiencing the guide through your physical five senses in the Physical Universe, similar to how you would perceive any living human being.

This is not the same as experiencing a *soul guide* or *spirit guide*, with your intuitive inner senses in the Nonphysical Universe, where you may know the soul closer to its pure essence.

The main difference is:

- If a soul guide showed itself to you *physically*, anyone would be able to see it.

- If it showed itself to you *nonphysically*, possibly only you would be able to see it.

Chapter 16

COMMUNICATE WITH SOULS AND THE SOURCE

There are numerous reasons why you would want to communicate and relate with your soul and Source guidance, or *guides*. By connecting with and developing a relationship with your guides, you may know all *answers*, understand all *wisdom*, and receive all *healing*.

The precise simplicity of living as a human is unimaginable to most people. It is really much easier than the world makes it out to be. Powerful you are, and how little you know just how powerful you can become. I intend to return your power to you, if you choose to listen and follow these simple instructions.

It begins with your choice to become the best. Being the best at something lies within every human and has been called passion, destiny, desire and many other words. Really it comes down to the law stating that every individual carries a unique facet of Divinity called the soul. This ensures your respect and dignity. Also, it maintains a consistent growth. Most importantly, a specialty lies within every human that if found and nurtured will create the human's unique and necessary part in the whole of Creation. This means that every human can be the best at something. It is a matter of clearing and finding it. The easiest way to accomplish this is through your relationship with your soul and Source guidance, which I simply call *guidance*.

Luckily for every human being, the ability to communicate with your guidance is innate and alive within all souls. This means you have the ability to communicate with me and your guidance, directly—right now.

There is no need for a middle person. There is no wall or barrier that is between you and your guidance unless you create it. If you have created walls, they can come down just as easily as they were created.

The only things that humans have no domain over changing are other souls and the Source. To put this into context, you can change almost anything in your reality with enough practice. Your guidance can show you how to practice and clear. They are the greatest resource available to you for *answers*, *insight* and *healing*. Use them. Use them every day. Use them in every way. Do not hesitate to use your guidance. Their purpose is to create with you. *Invite* them in now and *open* your life up to their assistance.

Beginning to use the innate wisdom within you is a great accomplishment. There are many that feel you must be gifted to be intuitive and communicate with God. I disagree. Everyone has this innate ability. I will show you how to use it.

Chapter 17

INTUITIVE INNER SENSES: THE FOUR QUALITIES

There are four main ways of *intuitive communication.* These *intuitive inner senses* include knowing, seeing, hearing and feeling. You have all four qualities, but you probably have some that are stronger and some that are weaker.

It is important to understand your four *intuitive inner senses*, which I will refer to as your *four qualities*, because they are the way in which you can telepathically communicate without words or physical movement. They are also useful for perceiving various aspects of Creation.

These four qualities are based on vibrations far above and beyond the vibrations of the Physical Universe. Because these ways of communication are not of the Physical Universe, they cannot be measured by physical means. You can detect other energies ignited by the four qualities. Still, your technology is not even close to this discovery, but it will be in the next one hundred years.

You will have technology you could not have dreamt of by the turn of the century. By the turn of the millennia, you will be traveling to other stars and solar systems in the blink of an eye. It is possible.

You will accomplish this if your planet survives the next twenty years. The next twenty years will decide the fate of your race.

- Will you restore balance to your world, or take it into a lower vibration?

The chance of survival is great, but there is still a consideration of extinction. With free will I can only intervene to a degree before I am living your lives for you. I will intervene as much as possible. However, you must make an active choice to face challenge and evolve through your differences, creating *opportunities* instead of *war*.

You will be pushed to great lengths to restore balance to this world and some will die. When this happens, rejoice and celebrate that the *new world* is coming and death will not be the same experience. In essence, you will experience immortality. Death will be a choice, and will be celebrated.

If you die, then die for your truth and as a free soul. Love life and love death. Celebrate Them Both. Then you will be open to the miracles that are possible.

Part of the balancing of this world is the restoring of your innate wisdom of who you are. It is mostly stripped away from people at birth, leaving little of your simple, pure nature. Let us explore this.

Even though a young child does not have their spiritual quadrant open and does not understand it, in most cases, until around adolescence, the child will be very aware of their spiritual nature. You could say they are living spirituality but have not yet deciphered it with their mind and explored the greater perspective of their soul's nature. Still, what is natural for them is condemned and condescended by adults, who do not understand the innate nature, mostly because they learned from their parents the same thing, namely, to condemn and condescend. Therefore, there is definitely a *pattern* to look at.

How can children feel okay with their natural spirituality from birth? Adults must shift their perspective.

One very significant part of returning to the innate balance is to reopen the four qualities, if they have been shut down. If an adult can do this, they can better understand the child and nurture the child's innate spiritual nature.

Chapter 18

INTUITIVE INNER SEEING

The *seeing quality* is essential in many respects, when living as a visionary or when relating to beauty and color.

One who has a strong *intuitive inner seeing quality* is known as a *seer*, or simply one who can see the Nonphysical Reality. This means, as a seer, you could see your guidance and energies that are invisible to the eye. You do this with your *inner imagination*, also known as your *third eye*, which is located at your sixth chakra. It allows you to see the Nonphysical Reality.

- A seer may have big, round eyes, and they will tend to be a prominent feature on the face.

- If you are a seer, you would be able to imagine very easily, and would tend to dream and daydream a lot.

- You would also see in picture form when someone is speaking with you, and before you conjure your thoughts, you may see a picture of what you will be saying.

- Seers have a natural ability for visualizing and creating their visions such as artists or interior designers.

- Other vocations and avocations would involve being around beautiful things and expressing yourself with beauty.

- The seer may close down their seeing if they experience something in their life, typically in childhood, that they don't want to see or remember. It could be anything really.

- *Seeing* is very important because when you visualize your goals and reality, you can manifest a powerful life. Imagination and visualization are incredible tools of creation. Remember this.

- If your seeing or any of the other qualities have been closed down, then use The Five Accomplishments to find out why and balance it.

- You may have been born with a weak seeing quality, and by exercising it, you will increase it to your desired strength.

In a balanced world, most people would be equally balanced with all four qualities.

➢ As you read these passages, you can determine the order of your four qualities. Number them in order, starting with one as the strongest quality and four as the weakest.

Also, if you think of each of the four qualities as an equal percentage, (25% + 25% + 25% + 25% = 100%), this would mean you are completely balanced and equal in all four qualities. You would still have an order from strongest to weakest. This order is to be looked at as natural, because everyone experiences the world differently.

For instance:

1. If you first experience the world through sight, seeing would be one.

2. If next you experience it through feeling, then feeling would be two.

3. And so on…

Even if you are equal, you will experience the world by the order of your qualities. Some people, with equal qualities, will switch their order around depending on what the situation requires. They may have one order when they are with their family and another order when they are at work. This is how the qualities are meant to function for most people. This way, a person has them balanced enough that they can bring in a quality as the situation requires.

DEVELOPING YOUR INTUITIVE INNER SEEING QUALITY

To increase and develop your seeing quality, please practice the following exercises:

- Admire the beauty of everything such as art and nature. Stare at its intricacies and see how necessary the *beauty* of your surroundings is to your *outlook* on life.

- When you shop for food, like produce, choose it by *how it looks*. When shopping for clothes, choose them by how they look on you.

- Care for and nurture your physical appearance, truly looking your best always, and admire yourself in the mirror as beautiful or handsome.

- Take on hobbies that have to do with your seeing quality like painting, knitting, gardening or anything where you are *visualizing* the end result and creating it.

- Give yourself permission to see, and expect God to open up your seeing quality. I will come to you in meditation. If you use the Chakra Clearing Meditation to first clear, I will show myself to you. This can be very exciting. Don't let your mind discount it. Be open and allow whatever is to unfold.

- Lay down once a day and take a journey. Start with something simple.

  Imagine yourself getting up and walking around the house or doing things at work. Imagine yourself at your favorite spots in nature and create new, special places in nature. Create more and more until you have a control over your imagination and can visualize at any time.

- Practice visualizing your goals and your self-image. You can heal yourself by visualizing yourself as whole and balanced. Dedicate yourself to owning your creative power of sight and have fun with it.

When using your seeing quality, you will not necessarily see as you do with your eyes. Many people think you will, but mostly you see with an intuitive inner sense.

- It is easier for some to close their eyes and imagine what they are seeing, whether it be a guide or simply energies.

- You may notice something out of the corner of your eye, and instead of looking directly at what you notice, look the other way and *imagine* what is there.

Please know that you may think you are making it up in your mind, but more than likely you are not making it up. To be sure you are clear, you may first clear yourself with the Chakra Clearing Meditation.

When seeing nonphysical experiences, note that the colors may be a different experience than with your eyes. The sights are phenomenal and breathtaking, once you get the hang of it.

When you see your guidance, they may come in many different forms. They will most likely come to you in a form that you are comfortable with. For some it is an animal or fairies. For others it may be a person or an angel with wings.

The true nature of your guidance is a *pure energy* that undulates with color and a sound, of sorts, that includes feelings and other senses unexplained until experienced. This means that the natural form a guide would take is a glob of energy, which may shimmer and sparkle with what I explained above.

Guides rarely take their natural form, for people wouldn't accept them if they did, and possibly would dismiss them as a figment of the imagination. Some people will only accept a guide in a certain form and so the guide will work within that form. Remember your guidance will work in whatever belief system you have, and it is not the name or form necessarily that is imperative, but rather the actions and examples the guidance shares. Therefore, you may see your guidance come to you in any form they feel you are comfortable with. There will be a time when your guidance comes to you as their pure, natural form and you will accept them as such. Until that time, see past the mask and costume they present, and seek the knowledge, wisdom and healing they have to share.

VISIONS AND DREAMS

The true nature of visions is a vehicle for your guidance to give you valuable and useful information for your and the world's evolution. Visions are not naturally invoked by a seer but rather initiated by the seer's guidance. *Visions* are part of the way your guidance navigates you through your destiny. In most cases, visions must use one of the other three qualities to interpret the significance and meaning of a vision. Visions are not the same as dreams.

Dreams are your personality's way of processing and evolving during sleep. It is very necessary to dream. Someone who does not remember their dreams would have an imbalance in their seeing quality. Every human dreams. It is part of the natural evolution of a human. You can use your dreams as a gauge of what is processing in your personality and what you are being exposed to that is affecting you.

Dreams can very easily be interpreted, unlike the complex systems people have created. The basic understanding of a dream is not only to identify what you see, but even more significantly, what you feel and what you think about what you feel. The seeing part of a dream is an attention getter, of sorts, and is not consistent from person to person. Dreams are as unique as every human's personality is unique. What you must remember from the dream is the significant emotions and thoughts behind each portion of the dream, in order to create a greater picture of what is taking place in your personality.

- When your perspective of your thoughts and emotions change, you dream about it.

- When you are overloaded mentally and emotionally, you can release it through dreaming.

The dreaming process was designed for the mental and emotional experiences of your physical life. Dreaming has nothing to do with your nonphysical or soul experiences.

For instance, if you dream about being chased and running away, what are the emotions and thoughts behind the dream? Maybe you feel that no matter what you do, people are always trying to get you or that there is no way out. Maybe you think it will never end, so in your dreams it doesn't ever end and you keep dreaming about the same thing.

Dream interpretation is not based so much on the seeing aspect, but mostly on the feeling and thinking aspects on a person-to-person basis. In the end, you can get very fluent at gauging how far you've come in clearing yourself with your dreams. You can gauge the clarity and health or balance of your personality by your dreams. Dreams were created for this sole purpose.

You may have visions while you are asleep and most would call these dreams, but they are not dreams, they are visions. If you have a vision in your sleep, it is because it is easier for your guidance to share the information with you in your sleep than when you are awake. The vision could be something that you need to change or do in your life.

Even though a dream and vision may seem very similar while sleeping, they are completely different. *Dreaming* is a simple process like your heart pumping blood. It does what it does automatically without an intelligence directing it. *Visions* are created by your guidance and are directed by your guidance.

Under the law of free will, you can control your dreams and visions. You can manipulate them if you desire. Manipulating your dreams would be self-defeating and would create an imbalance in your personality over time. You would essentially be creating against the natural processes of your evolvement. If you manipulate visions, you will be interrupting the clarity of the message your guidance is sharing with you. In a vision you will be interacting to a degree. However, it is important to let the vision play its course and not fear it or change it significantly. Allow your guidance to share what they are intending to share.

MATERIALIZATION

If your guidance is appearing physically to you, then you are using your eyes to perceive them. Your guidance can come to you physically in several ways:

- The most common is as an *ethereal form* or *etherealization*, which is seen as a subtle, transparent, usually white energy. Note that this form is physical energy that the guide has created to show itself to you.

- The other form, which is very rare in this time of the world, is *materialization*. This means your guide would create a physical body just like yours with few differences.

A *materialized form* is basically a physical human body with blood, hair and everything else that a healthy physical body has. This type of contact is almost nonexistent without the help of a special group of participants.

This has happened, for example, when masters from the past have died and revisited their disciples as a physical, materialized form. A materialized guide can do anything that you can do because they take on a human physical form.

There are many stories of this throughout your religious texts. Most commonly is the story of a man who lived around 2000 years ago. He is in many of your history and religious texts. He did, in fact, materialize after he died and met with his followers to further guide them with his teachings. This, of course, was to also prove the continuity of life in that the soul is eternal and exists after your body dies.

There have been stories about special groups of people who gather to welcome their guidance as materialized forms. There are still some groups in the world today, but most of them are kept hidden for fear of what the world would say and do to them. It was extremely common about 200,000 years ago and even widely practiced as recently as 50,000 years ago, but as you can see, the reality of it has not been known for quite some time. I am returning this very natural practice of celebrating and communing with your guidance in materialized forms.

You will experience this phenomenon in every government body and source of power and guidance for the world's future. In time all will experience materialized guidance, and it will be as natural as calling someone on the phone or seeing a friend you haven't seen in awhile. Imagine when you can once again see and physically be with your family or friends who died. Let us then welcome this experience into the world, once again, and return a long lost practice to our hearts where it belongs. I will teach you how to do this in later books as groups. For now simply create the experience by embracing the idea of it being possible.

Life after death will be proven scientifically soon as a result of materialization. When this happens, a much needed shift in the world's perspective will occur, and you will witness one of the greatest milestones in the evolution of Earth. This is truly something to fantasize and look forward to.

SPLITTING YOUR CONSCIOUSNESS

There are other dimensions to your seeing quality that pertain to the Nonphysical Universe. You are able to use it to view the world without your eyes. This is called by many names which include *remote viewing*, *astral travel* and *out of body travel.*

The clearest way to experience this type of intuitive seeing is by *splitting your consciousness*, rather than your *consciousness leaving your body.*

Accurately speaking, your consciousness is *grounded* in your body, yet you are aware of another location at the same time.

Therefore, I recommend for you not to leave your body. You don't ever need to leave your body while you are awake to accomplish an experience. I am dispelling the myth that you need to leave your body, as with out of body travel and astral travel. Remote viewing typically requires one to stay grounded, and in most cases requires some elaborate model of identifying your target location. The simple idea of splitting your consciousness to another location requires no model, though it does require *clarity* and *practice*.

What you are doing when you split your consciousness is remaining conscious and aware of where your body is, and at the same time becoming conscious and aware of another location where your body is not. In actuality, you may split your consciousness as many times as you choose.

The important point is to stay grounded. If you can be grounded and split your consciousness, you will actually have a greater power over your experience than if you are not grounded. Being *grounded* is your *point of power*, as it is when you are facilitating a balanced physical experience. This means that with enough practice, you can actually create another body in a different location or affect the physical location just as you would if your body was there.

Your effectiveness in any location where you split your consciousness to is determined by how grounded and focused you are. The clearer you are, the more focused you will be, and as a result, the more creative force you will have.

What really determines effectiveness in your reality is your belief that certain laws hold this Physical Universe together. You have determined that if you throw a rock in the air it will fall down because of gravity. If your belief that the rock would hover is *stronger* than your belief that it will fall, you would create the rock to hover. There is nothing simpler than creation. It starts with your beliefs.

1. Look at and determine what beliefs are holding you back from becoming the master of your reality. What is limiting you?

2. Then, go forward to dismantle and dissect your beliefs until you can sincerely change them to something that embraces all possibility. By doing this, you have taken a step forward into becoming the true being that you are.

3. This will take practice and you will need to practice every day, hopefully all the time.

If you truly want to master your life, then please practice the techniques in this book and look forward to the freedom you will have as a result of it.

Remember, at the end of your life, it will be the challenges you faced and trials you endured that you will celebrate. The greatest challenges bring the greatest rewards and will always reap the greatest celebrations.

Thank you for considering all you may become.

Chapter 19

INTUITIVE INNER KNOWING

Knowing is the one quality related to your *soul.* Unlike the other three qualities, knowing is not related to a physical aspect of your personality: the seeing quality relates to sight and dreams, the hearing quality relates to sound and thoughts, and the feeling quality relates to touch and emotions.

The knowing quality functions on a different level of consciousness than the other three. It is called *prophecy* because knowing is *instant* and *without reason.* It simply is what it is and you know it. To understand knowing is impossible because it is not a quality of understanding.

Another important quality is your *hearing quality* because it is what *organizes* and creates *order* with your other two qualities of seeing and feeling. The hearing quality is the most versatile because it puts everything in life together and makes sense of it all.

The *knowing quality* is the most useful because it is a *direct connection*, of sorts, to the soul and requires little analyzing to become confident in your answers and guidance.

If your knowing is imbalanced, you will react on it without any regard of how or when your thoughts are presented. This type of person has been called the know-it-all and can be challenging to be around. The imbalanced knower will take over conversations and butt into situations obtrusively.

Also, an imbalance in the knowing can create a shutdown of confidence and result in very low self-esteem. Knowing is confidence, and an imbalance can be *overconfidence* or *underconfidence*.

Either way, it is detrimental to your personality to have an imbalance in the knowing quality. The imbalance would affect your interpretation of the world in every way including relationships, career and your connection with God. The knowing quality is your invisible line to your soul and the Source.

It requires you to be confident in your ability to live. So when the knowing quality is imbalanced, you will experience a lack of will to live. You will tend to focus primarily on how you may stay connected to your perspective instead of changing.

When you are in touch with your knowing quality in a *balanced* way, you will experience several things:

- An awareness that is all-encompassing of both *knowledge* and *wisdom.*

- A sense of *peace* inside created from the realization of your *true purpose* and *connection* with God.

- An ability to use your knowing quality to *reinforce the other three qualities* in a confident and humble way.

- You will experience *humbleness*, which is very rare.

When your knowing quality is *out of balance*:

- You experience *judgment*, because humbleness is a result of being connected and aligned with the soul's clear perspective of love. Whereas, judgment brings one a sense of rigid attachments to the way things are or must be.

- The person would feel a *severed connection* with the soul, metaphorically speaking, because of the unclear personality.

- The personality would be focused on *being right* and maintaining a comfort level, resulting in the person missing the most important part of living—Change.

Ideally you will have a balanced knowing quality so you can navigate through the world in a confident way. As one balances the personality, they will have a clearer knowing perspective.

Understand that knowing is the one quality that is dependent on the clarity of the personality for effectiveness. Again, this is directly related to the alignment of the soul with the personality. Still, I include it with the other three qualities to give you a working relationship of the four together.

If you have not received The Initiation, then your knowing is not balanced. It is directly related to your alignment with your soul's clear love. Once you balance your personality, and thereby your knowing quality, you will be the master at anything you set your mind to do.

Confidence is the most essential part of the personality next to humility. Under humility lie many wonderful qualities. *Humility* is the embodiment of *equality* and *oneness*. Humility is not the same as compassion, but you might say it is a result of compassion, which is a result of a clear perspective of love.

A *humble knower* is the most powerful personality type available to humans. A humble knower, or in other words a *balanced knower*, will empower people and manifest clear truth, love and the light of their soul in everything they do.

Great masters have all been knowers because it takes a knower to be able to confidently create the miracles and episodes that occurred during their lives.

Look back on your life as a knower and ask yourself if your experiences are from an *underconfidence*, *overconfidence* or *balanced confidence*. This will identify to you where you can work on yourself in order to bring in this great power to your personality.

The importance is great, so please pay attention to the above paragraphs on *knowing* and work hard to *clear* yourself.

DEVELOPING YOUR INTUITIVE INNER KNOWING QUALITY

To increase and develop your confidence and knowing quality, please practice the following exercises:

- Become more capable with the other three qualities of feeling, seeing and hearing.
- Get up in the morning and look at yourself in the mirror and say, "I am such a wonderful person" and such things as "I am beautiful and confident."

- You may use confident words like "*know*," and affirm things as a matter of fact.

  For instance, instead of saying, "I *think* I'll do this" or "I *might* do this" with uncertainty, say, "I *am* going to do this" or "I *know* this is what I am to do" with certainty.

  Certainty is what you say and also the *energy* behind the words.

- To balance overconfidence, you must *embrace humility* by bowing down to other's perspectives and not having to be right or make a point. Let others speak their mind and genuinely try to understand their perspective.

- Also, give yourself *permission to change your perspective*. Know that your perspective is not the only or best one for you. Your perspective will change as you evolve. If you attach to your perspective, as an overconfident knower does, you will not change and will not evolve. The essence of change is to first recognize your perspective will change. How can you change if your perspective does not change?

Get out of the energy of proving yourself and needing to be heard. *Embrace* the energy of *learning* from others and remembering your *soul's perspective*. *Love* will always lift the hardest of hearts to joy if one is open to change. Love yourself enough to allow yourself to change. Whether you are overconfident or underconfident, you will benefit from the openness to change.

Chapter 20

INTUITIVE INNER HEARING

As mentioned before, the *hearing quality* is the most versatile of the four qualities and deserves the greatest attention to understand, because it will create your overall perspective on life.

Balancing the other qualities will be done through the hearing quality. It is the source of your *truth* and the *root* of every aspect of your personality.

The hearing quality was created so you may facilitate a human experience and have a glue to hold it all together. Without the hearing quality, you would not have a context to create continuity in time or space.

The mind is directly related to the hearing quality as the eyes are related to the seeing quality or the emotions are related to the feeling quality. It is your hearing quality that intends and organizes the beliefs that you have learned in life. In order to change your reality, you must find the root belief with The Five Accomplishments and change it. There are other experiences coalesced with your beliefs, but it is beliefs that are creating your reality and it is beliefs that must be changed for you to evolve.

Therefore, you will be working primarily with your thoughts and how they form beliefs to increase and focus the creative power of your knowing quality.

- The *power* is the knowing, which is confidence.

- The *direction* of that power is the hearing, which is thoughts, beliefs and intention.

Learn to *navigate* with your hearing and learn to *propel* with your knowing.

- Hearers tend to have beady eyes, much more narrow than a seer does.

- A person with balanced knowing and hearing makes a very successful businessperson or leader.

- Hearers would be attracted to pursuits of the mind like reading, tinkering, traveling and learning.

- You might find a hearer in vocations and avocations such as engineering, science, accounting and other forms of problem solving and number crunching.

- A very strong hearer may seem emotionless. It would then be important for them to open up their feeling quality to balance the strong hearing.

- Things need to make sense to a strong hearer; otherwise, many times, they cannot accept them.

When your hearing is balanced, it will connect and strengthen the rest of your personality. If one has relied on their hearing for most of their personality, then it must be balanced to be able to evolve into a clear perspective of love.

Someone may have the mind working overtime or undertime, and it is meant to be working in *present time* and balanced.

➢ Please consider the degree you use your hearing quality. Is it *balanced*, *overused* or *underused*?

If it is overused or underused, you may not be able to make a decision.

- *Overuse* of the mind will result in anxiety or worry, and possibly getting lost in the great philosophy of life.

- *Underuse* of the mind will result in not being able to understand and rationalize experiences.

Both underusing and overusing the hearing quality will leave a person frustrated and in fear, because if the hearing is not balanced that means you are not experiencing clear love and must use The Five Accomplishments.

As mentioned earlier, the four qualities are meant to be equal, though you will still have an order of preferability that may change depending on the situation. If you understand that they must be equal for you to conceive clear love and live from it, then you will have a gauge to go by when acknowledging your qualities and their order.

Your order is significant, as it will determine the main areas of career and inspiration you are drawn toward.

Education has been primarily dependent on the hearing quality, and this provides a great challenge to students. For education to be successful, it must embrace the mirror of a natural balanced personality using seeing, feeling, knowing and hearing—*equally*. However, education is not embracing this mirror. In fact, the very thought of asking a student how they *feel* about something would be unheard of, in most cases. To go further, there is no visualization or work on the confidence and intuitive inner knowing of a student. Instead, the student is told to remember and organize concepts that will be necessary in their field of study. This is one of the most imbalanced approaches to education.

Students are not taught and do not understand the correlation of the four qualities with their field of study. This is one of the most imperative teachings to be given. If you truly embrace a new way of teaching and learning, you will change your world in <u>one generation</u>. It is that simple. Do your part and make a change today.

When developing your hearing quality, you can best accommodate a balance by first watching your *thoughts* and *self-talk*. Your thoughts are powerful. Be aware of every thought happening in your mind. This will give you a control over your creations. If you are not aware of your thoughts and what they are creating, you will feel like a *victim* and that life is hard. Life is meant to be simple and fun, even during the most challenging times. If it is not, then analyze with your mind what thoughts are, either *subconsciously* or *consciously*, creating your reality.

You will indeed have *ninety percent* of your creations originating from your subconscious thinking. Your subconscious thoughts were learned, more than likely, in the *first six years* of your life and are manifesting your reality.

Subconscious thoughts may take a lifetime for some to explore and control. When I say *control*, I mean you will be aware and have a *choice* of what your subconscious thinking will create, rather than being controlled by those thoughts.

Most people are unaware of their subconscious thinking. You will use The Five Accomplishments to get to the root of your subconscious thoughts and change them to thoughts that are in accord with your soul's destiny. You will also transform your wants and desires to be in agreement with your soul's destiny.

- If you learned when you were four years old that it is not okay to speak out unless you were spoken to, you would want to find the root of that thought and change it or you might be challenged when expressing your truth.

- If you learned that you will be physically punished if you don't do what you are told, you might experience abusive relationships in your life.

- If when you disagreed, an adult punished you for your disagreement, this would create a subconscious thought in you to have low self-esteem and a thought that "The world is not a safe place." This, in turn, would create experiences in your life that would validate the subconscious thoughts.

The thoughts you learn and believe are the very essence of your *creative power*.

1. Be aware of what you are creating.

2. If you are not creating what you want, then look at your subconscious thoughts and beliefs.

Everyone in this world requires counseling with The Five Accomplishments to free themselves of their parents' or caretakers' beliefs. It is mandatory that this be practiced in schools, businesses, families and governments. In truth, everyone will benefit from the reorganizing and changing of their subconscious thinking.

Your *conscious thinking* is the most important. If you do not agree consciously that there is an imbalance in your subconscious thinking, you may walk in a stupor your entire life, never asking or inviting assistance to help you change.

Many feel there is no work to do on themselves and this is their choice. However, if you are one of these people, please wake up out of your slumber and grow. You will never grow until you acknowledge there is growth that can be done.

Note that every person who has ever and will ever live physically requires growth. *Growth* is the very essence of Creation. You exist to evolve in every experience and to expand Creation. To believe that you need no evolution is to believe against the very reason there is Creation and Earth.

1. Monitor your conscious thinking.

2. If you experience thoughts or self-talk that is creating against what you want or know is your soul's destiny, then demand of yourself a change.

3. Immediately put your intention into finding and changing the root thought that is creating against what you want.

There is a huge imbalance on this planet regarding people who blatantly know what is imbalanced and uncomfortable and continue to ignore the *indicators*.

1. *Take Responsibility* for your soul's journey on Earth.

2. *Observe*.

3. *Embrace*.

4. *Change* any thoughts that are not in harmony with your highest evolution.

I am looking at the bigger picture of a world that is content with their eyes half open. You will suffer and life will be challenging if you blatantly disobey your covenant with your soul's destiny.

You are the most challenged in this lifetime, out of any lifetime, because of the *energy* and *consciousness shift* that is among you. In this time, you have the greatest opportunity for evolution out of your soul's entire history of physical lives. Seize this opportunity; for if you do, there will be a great celebration when you physically die and return home.

Let us celebrate our accomplishments and let us embrace and love our challenges together.

You are responsible for most experiences that come into your life, so if there are experiences that are not understandable, please understand them by using The Five Accomplishments. To concur with many religious leaders throughout history, I acknowledge the fact that there is a great sacrifice to live for God and, in other words, live in service to your soul's destiny. The sacrifice is the responsibility that is felt when you decide to evolve instead of sloppily maintaining a certain comfort. Then you will reap the greatest reward. I believe in you . . . I encourage you to dance instead of sitting this one out.

Your hearing quality can be shut down for many reasons. One reason is your *self-worth*, which also affects your knowing quality. If your self-worth was imbalanced when you were a child, it will affect both your knowing and hearing qualities. It will affect your hearing in that you will retreat into your mind and build your life stronger in the mental realm because it was not okay for you to reveal and be safe with your emotions. This would amplify your hearing quality and create an underconfident knower. Your hearing would then be your coping mechanism and would drive your entire life. It would tell you when you can accept yourself and when you cannot. It would also tell you when you can express yourself and when you cannot. In fact, your hearing quality would become your friend, and most likely your feeling quality would become feared or even hated. This would lead to many other imbalances in your total personality.

If you learned that you *need to make sense* out of things in order to accept them, then your hearing would have a great imbalance because sometimes things don't always have a logical reason. You may have been taught that you *need to know why* and so everything you do you question, and you never stop questioning. You may question so much that it drives you crazy, and with a low knowing you might rarely come to a conclusion or decision. This would mean that you are going to find great hardship and worry. You may make a decision and because of this imbalance you would question whether you made the right choice or not. This would create great anxiety and in some cases a nervous breakdown, as some therapists have called it.

You would also think ahead and have trouble staying present with life. If you are trying to figure things out before they happen, it can cause a great stress and even physical headaches. To be rethinking the past and thinking about the future takes you directly out of the present, and will tend to *unground* you. By doing this, you are not accepting yourself and in most cases you do not accept others, and therefore you will struggle precariously. This type of person has been known as the basket case or one who does not have a handle on life. This is because they are not in life, but rather in the future or past. Please correct this imbalance in order to live and function in a loving way.

Let me explain the distinction between the *past* and the *future*. It is absolutely fundamental for your evolution to stay grounded in the *present* or you will find great imbalance in all areas of your life.

- The *past* was created to learn from, though if you return to it obsessively to regret and regurgitate the same things over and over, you will not evolve or benefit. You will take away from your life.

The *future* was designed to create goals and points of reference to return to, in an attempt to redirect your life's purpose. If you abuse the future, as most do, then you will find yourself attempting to control it, rather than use it as a guide. The future was not designed to control for it has within it infinite possibilities.

If you spend your time figuring out the various possibilities, you will drive yourself crazy, and in the least of circumstances, you will confuse yourself. It is very easy to confuse the human mind, if you have a pattern of confusion as many on this world do. You are, in effect, a very capable race of people, but because of the confusion many of you do not embrace changes. You are spending your time in the future trying to figure out what is about to take place, instead of being in the *moment* and planning how to evolve yourself and do your soul's work. Please release the past and the future, and use them only in special situations, when it is necessary. This is the essence of life, and to honor life, you honor your power in the present.

Another imbalance in the hearing quality stems from when children learn beliefs that motivate them to *be like someone else*. This is not imbalanced unless the belief is taken into a fear-based perspective. One such belief is that in order to succeed and live, you must be like Mom and Dad or be like the one who is accomplishing, in most cases, what the parents or caretakers hold as virtuous.

It is a great virtue to look to others and aspire to balance an aspect of yourself by receiving a role model's great inspiration. This is how we can share and grow together.

It is altogether different when it is expected of a child to mold like another, especially against their choice. This is called control and comes from insecurity in the adults. What you will expect to see with such a belief is that the child will not find their own identity and will wander around life trying to find it. It isn't until someone points them *within* themselves, to their soul's destiny, that they will find themselves.

It is important to keep a balance when teaching children about how and what to become, because if they learn they must become like others to gain acceptance and be loved, this will create a *need to please* in the individual. This affects the knowing quality by them looking for confidence outside of themselves. It also affects the hearing quality because they overanalyze their own opinion and question whether what they are doing is right or not.

The hearing quality, in its natural, balanced form, would be used when organizing experiences or thoughts. The hearing quality has been put into *overuse* or *underuse* by imbalances, creating an effect of *stress* or *unreasoning* respectively.

Features of the hearing quality include an *inner voice* that may be heard as your voice or another voice in your mind. It's different than hearing with your physical ears.

If you are hearing the voice in your mind, then others will not be able to hear the voice, unless they are picking it up with their intuitive hearing as well. You will get words or concepts that come into your mind as thoughts. As you do, they may turn into a voice and eventually a clear dialogue with your guidance.

Using your four qualities, you can send and receive with another person. The four qualities were designed as your most natural form of communication with your guidance and other people. The languages of Earth were created by humans, and there are so many, whereas the four qualities were created by the Source. There is a huge difference.

In the interim transition of old and new worlds, design a combination of *spoken word* and the *four qualities* that will broaden the perspective of communication with each other. With this, even if you do not speak the same language as another, you will be able to communicate.

CHANNELED WRITING (AUTOMATIC WRITING)

A form of communication through the hearing quality is *subconscious writing* or *channeled writing*. You have called it *automatic writing*. It is where your guidance comes through your subconscious mind and communicates with you through writing. This form of communication with your guidance is seen as a great avenue for those who are still strengthening their four qualities to clarity.

This form of writing is very common in many who don't realize they are channeling their guidance. Most of the well-known books that have inspired people were channeled in this form.

The reason for this type of writing is to give you a tool that you can use anywhere and at anytime.

CHANNELED WRITING EXERCISE

1. To start, please use a paper and writing utensil that is comfortable for you.

2. Know that the writing is not going to happen on its own. It is closer to an *inspired writing*, rather than expecting your guidance to physically pick up the writing utensil and move your hand around the page.

3. Write a question on the page and expect to receive the answer.

4. Don't think about the answer. Just let it pop into your mind, and when you get a sense of the first few words, start writing them down.

5. As you write half a page to a page, you will fall into a very *inspired feeling* that will seem to be writing without your thought of it.

6. The guidance is coming through your mind so it will seem like it is you. The difference will be the flow, and

after you practice enough, you will notice the way you write may change. You may use different words and sentence structure than you normally would.

Embrace channeled writing and teach it to your children so they may learn and understand their life. Their minds have so many questions and if they learn to use this form of problem solving, it can save much time and frustration for the adult.

CHANNELED WRITING ACCURACY

The most important part of this process is to *trust* that it is not you.

Wait until you are completely done writing before you judge whether it is accurate or not. Many people talk themselves out of the accuracy, and stop altogether, because they think it is coming from their mind. It is coming through the mind, so believe that it is not you and it is your guidance.

Also, your guidance is always putting thoughts into your mind to direct you. If you receive something similar to what has been in your mind, please don't disregard it. It could very well be the same thing that your guidance has been trying to get across to you. They will use any means to communicate with you and redirect you onto your soul's destiny.

To be as clear as you can with your messages, *let go* of needing the answer to be a certain way and tell God, "I give my wants and desires to you. Please tell me what is in my best interest or highest benefit. Thank you." If you truly mean it when you say it, you will receive clear answers.

When you desire to communicate using your hearing quality, your mind must be as *clear* as possible from your wants and desires because you can program the result of the answer with your mind. This is very easy to do. Use the Chakra Clearing Meditation to clear your energy, and especially your mind, so that you may truly give your wants and desires to God and receive messages clearly without distorting it with your mind.

If your mind is still overactive, use The Five Accomplishments and increase the other three qualities to compensate.

Your *intention* is imperative when communicating with your guidance. Absolutely know, without a doubt, you will connect and receive exactly what you need for your life in the moment you are asking. Any communicated information is relevant for the time and situation it is in. The information may change by the very nature of Creation which is change. You can be certain that the information you receive is to be taken as truth for the circumstances when it is received.

Channeling is of the hearing quality. *Channeling* is when your guidance comes into your *energy field* and shares your field with you. Then they speak through your mind and voice.

This gives the appearance that your body is taken over and the feeling of possession; however, two beings cannot possess one body. It is impossible under many universal laws. It may feel like the being possesses the body, though this is not true. The person who is channeling the being is always in control, unless there is a thought that they would like the experience of possession. Then, the channel can create such an experience. If this happens, it is a projection of the channel and not an act of the being. Just as when a channel changes their voice or does any number of rituals that are normal with many channels, it is of the person's belief system and not of the need for doing so.

I want to make a clear distinction between a *belief of the mind* and a *universal truth*. As mentioned earlier, you can create any number of thoughts that can be as real as anything in your physical experience. The crucial point is to remember this, you can fool yourself into thinking there are harmful beings that want to hurt you, if that is what you learned as a child. Many people have learned such a thing. To make matters worse, there are millions of words in countless books that support the belief of *negative* or *evil* beings that will hurt you or at least disturb you. Many of your most authentic, known religious and spiritual writers have written about such untruths.

The truth is there is no spiritual energy that is unclear. All *spiritual energy*, which is souls and the Source, is *pure love energy*, and you will experience such if your beliefs are clear. Anything other than this is created by your mind and would need The Five Accomplishments to clear.

You have nothing to fear when experiencing your guidance. You will grow and evolve into the beautiful being you are. Please open up to your fears and clear them.

DEVELOPING YOUR INTUITIVE INNER HEARING QUALITY

To increase and develop your hearing quality, please practice the following exercises:

- *Read* and *think* about what you have read. *Analyze* it and *remember* it.

- When you buy something, think about whether you will use it and how. Compare prices and analyze what the best deal is.

- Before acting on something think about it. Think about the big picture and how what you are about to do fits into the larger picture.

- Use phrases like, "I *hear* what you are saying." or "I'll *think* about that." when you are communicating.

- You could take a class or hobby related to the intellect such as science, math, philosophy and literature. Focus on subjects where you are analyzing what you have studied. This will help you to increase your hearing quality.

- You may also use exercises that focus your creative thoughts. Put a thought out to the Universe and see how long it takes for you to receive the experience. When you do receive something, follow it back to the root thought that created it.

When you have a command over your thoughts and how they are creating, you are the center of your creation. When you put your responsibility outside of yourself and subject yourself as a victim of the universe, you are disempowered and are going to struggle. Live life free and responsibly. Then you will align with your soul's love. It is a matter of acknowledging your power and truly living it.

Concentrate on your evolution and stay with it no matter how challenging things become. God is always with you, most of all, when you feel it the least. The most challenging times will bring you the greatest opportunity to return to your *innocence*. Your guidance is waiting patiently for recognition so they may assist you.

Unbending intention is a thought that does not waiver. Most individuals have wavering thoughts. They may create a thought of wanting to accomplish something, and then days or even moments later, they create another thought that says they cannot accomplish it or that there will be obstacles. This *wavering intention* may have little to no power and is creating against you. An *unbending intention* is a thought or thoughts that you believe in and focus so well that they do not change, until you *consciously* decide they will. The more focused you become, the greater power you will have in directing your thoughts. This relates to your knowing and hearing qualities, and the two balanced together create an unbending intention.

You may refine your focus to the degree of manifesting physical things out of thin air and levitating. It is when you reach this clarity that you are truly at the *center of Creation*, giving your mind control over physical matter. There are laws that govern this, and as you ascend into this clarity, you will become aware of how and what to create, and when to create it. With this clarity comes an awareness of the Source, and as this happens you will walk with the Source. Very rarely does one achieve this clarity without The Initiation. If you have achieved this clarity, then you are certainly aligned with your soul.

The mind is a fascinating invention and one that deserves respect. Many in this world do not revere their mind but rather blaspheme it because of the imbalances. The only way to succeed in changing your mind is to first *embrace* it. The mind is a tool and is to be looked at as such. It is your creative tool. Sharpen and nurture it. Then wield it with respect and humility.

Before I speak about the feeling quality, know that the meaning of this section on the four qualities is to give you a realization of your inner workings. There have been so many subjects taught and talked about, and books written on the inner workings of a human being, yet few have clearly touched on the innate nature of the personality of a human. The four qualities are the inner workings of a human and will tell you everything you need to know about their behavior and makeup.

Please consider these teachings as a replacement for many fields including psychology, medicine and healing. If you do not switch and embrace these teachings all at once, please do so at a pace that is comfortable, for they will make it much easier for this world to function.

Reach the world through your intuitive inner qualities and touch the world with your soul.

In the end, recognize there is much more to life than what this world has thought. In fact, there is much more than I have disclosed. Even as controversial as this book is, there are still things I am not revealing yet, as it would be premature and useless if you don't first recognize the usefulness in these initial teachings. Thank you again for your consideration of such drastic changes in thinking.

Chapter 21

INTUITIVE INNER FEELING

I will speak of your *feeling quality* and its addition to your total personality. Feelings and emotions were created to give you *depth* to your experiences. If it were not for emotions, you would not focus and notice a *change*.

Emotions tell you where to go next by *indicating* imbalances and balances in your perspective of love. *Emotions* are indeed the strongest *indicators* that you have to change your course in life. They indicate whether you perceive clear love. They encourage you to evolve, and in doing so, they are your *greatest tool for evolution*.

All emotions are *neutral* and of *equal importance*. All must be *embraced* and looked at as treasures, because they give your life depth and show you where to go next in your evolution. Emotions are your roadmap to fulfilling your destiny, and if used accurately, you may evolve right out of the need to return physically.

Emotional imbalances cause most people to become incapacitated physically. *Physical imbalances* are primarily created from emotions, and in some instances directly from the mind. The mind creates the experience of emotions, which if imbalanced, creates physical imbalance in the body.

Rarely will the body pick up an imbalance that has no relation to the mind or emotions. However, there could be an environmental factor such as radiation or pollution. Even so, the mind is strong enough to counter any environmental factors, short of total annihilation of the physical body.

Emotions are vibrationally located between thoughts and the physical body, and are a direct result of thoughts. When emotional energy is not expressed and accepted, it is repressed and stored in the physical body. This can create a physical imbalance like cancer or any other classified disease.

Disease is nothing more than an *indicator* showing you something that deserves attention.

1. Listen and shift the root of the indicator.

2. It will then have no reason to exist.

3. And the disease will go away.

Diseases are terminal when a person ignores what the indicator is showing them.

FEELINGS VERSUS EMOTIONS

Nonphysical *feelings* are different than *emotions. Feelings* can be associated with your guidance, soul or another human communicating something with you. They use emotional energy. Though instead of originating from your mind like emotions, they originate from another being like your guidance, soul or a person, and pass through your mind.

In rare cases feelings can be so powerful that they create a *physical presence* and can be felt physically without passing through your mind. Then they would be closer to a physical experience, than one of a nonphysical feeling quality.

It would be similar to being out in the sun and feeling the heat wave. It is energy, but one of the *physical* rather than the *nonphysical.* Such energies can be measured with physical instruments.

To clarify, if you have nonphysical feelings moving in your energy field, they cannot be directly measured; whereas if the nonphysical feeling is so powerful that it manifests a physical feeling, it can be measured. An example would be if your guide physically touched your skin, compared to a nonphysical feeling sensation as a wave of tingly energy.

The point is your guidance does convey messages through your feeling quality in any number of ways:

- They can give you a *gut feeling*.

- *Tingles* or *chills*.

- You may also receive *hot* or *cold* energy that is unexplained.

- Guidance has been known to physically *brush up against* people.

- They may help to invoke a certain *emotion* in you.

The *healing energy* your guidance pours into you is through your feeling quality. If you are open to it, your guidance can heal anything mentally, emotionally or physically.

It is amazing the diverse methods your guidance use to help you evolve. One very common way of getting your attention is to pull your energy in a particular direction. Like the times you felt to look or move in a direction, only to find something or someone you needed to be aware of; or when you felt as if you should do something or not do it. In these types of situations, you are using your feeling quality.

With your feelings you can *sense* someone's presence in a room you are in, or if you are sensitive enough, you can sense them at great distances. This also is true with your guidance.

Feelings can *empower thoughts* just as imagination can. If you use your feelings with your knowing and hearing, you will be more powerful. It dynamically gives your thoughts more weight to move into the physical.

Like thoughts, clear and focused feelings will be a great asset to your *creative power*. You are a creator by nature, so anything you can do to refine your creativity is desired.

Strong feelers can notice the *emotions left in a location.* For example, if a couple has been arguing and their friend comes over, who is a strong feeler, the friend will sense the angry energy left from the argument, and might feel uncomfortable in it. This holds true with any emotion including the *five main emotions* of love, anger, jealousy, fear and grief.

A feeler will also be *emotional*, tending to cry or laugh easily.

There are more feelers than there are seers because the feeling quality is your experience of life in the deepest impacting way. Everything that tells you something about yourself is felt. You feel and by feeling, you are able to grow, evolve and navigate through your lessons. If it wasn't for the feeling quality, you would be stagnant and remain in a stasis with your evolution.

Those who shut down their emotions or learn to express them in an imbalanced way during childhood are more likely to feel the impact of the feeling quality, than those that have a balanced feeling quality. The reason that *pain* is felt by emotional imbalances is because of the *inability to receive love.* When one has blocked themselves from receiving love, they feel pain. This is the only time a person feels pain other than physical trauma.

UNCONDITIONAL LOVE

You must really understand love and its misconceptions. You, who are sharing love clearly, will do so for the purpose of sharing it without any intention of receiving. If there is an intention of receiving something for the love you share, then it is not love, it is manipulation or prostitution. You put a vessel of love out for someone with a string attached to it and a larger empty vessel next to it expecting it to be filled and returned. If your larger vessel is not filled, then you pull back the love you gave and block the exchange from being completed.

Many think they feel love but are really saying, "You please me. You please me because you do this for me and it makes me happy."

- ➢ What if the person stopped pleasing? Would you still love them?

- Would you love your partner if they stopped cooking dinner or stopped bringing in a certain income?

- Would you love them if they changed and were not the same person anymore?

- Is your love conditional?

Pure love is given for the simple pleasure of giving. If what you give is for any other reason, consider clearing your blocks. Block yourself from giving love freely and you will suffer and feel pain emotionally, mentally and physically. There are agreements you make with others and this is fine; however, above all other agreements must be *love without conditions*.

There is an imbalanced interpretation of how to receive love; it shows one receiving love through abuse or by going along with whatever another person does to them. Love yourself and decide what energy you will have in your presence. <u>You can love someone and disagree</u>, but this does not mean you must be in their proximity or even speak with them. You are a sovereign being, and as such, you will choose a direction and company that suits your destiny. In doing so, you may show *equality* and *love* in everything you do and not judge those you disagree with. It is very important to give others the *respect* that you deserve.

To recap from an earlier section in the book, under the law of oneness and equality, everything is love and one. Under the law of free will and other laws pertaining to the individuality of the soul, you will also have an identity and your identity will share and receive differently than every other soul on Earth. Therefore, know that people are doing the best they can to share clear love, and the best service to yourself is to receive their love however they are able to share it.

If a friend only knows love by giving you a card, then that is their way, whereas another friend may show love by giving you a hug and asking you how your day went. Both are *equally* valuable and should both be respected.

Another person may show love by beating another person in a relationship. Their expression of love, even as unclear as it is, must also be respected, for it is the best way they know how to share love, given their life experiences. Under many universal laws, such as self-preservation, the person abused must leave the proximity of the abuser and find a relationship that shows them more respect. The choice is theirs, and if they choose to stay, it is because they don't love themselves or the person that is abusing them. What they are really experiencing is *fear*.

People in abusive relationships have often chosen to stay in them because of what they call love. It is not because of love that they stay but rather a lack of love. Please respect others for how they are able to show love.

Many find the difference between *love* and *fear* is perspective, and this is true, to a degree. There is a very clear distinction between the two.

Love is acceptance.

Fear is unacceptance.

It is very simple. All experiences come from these two main emotions. When you *accept*, you have nothing to fear and you live *free*.

Anger is the most misunderstood emotion. It is a tool and a valuable one. Let me add anger with other emotions you experience. They are beneficial because they show you something. Pay attention to what they show you and make a change either within yourself or outside in your physical world. You will then be using emotions as they were designed.

- A feeler likes to *work with their hands* in their vocation or avocations.

- A feeler will be a natural at pursuits such as sculpting, drafting, carpentry, cooking, healing, massage and other hands-on skills.

- They exude love and typically want to *be of service* to humanity. You might find a feeler involved in humanitarian efforts or charities.

- Feelers are commonly doctors, nurses and veterinarians or work in other careers associated with healing and helping people.

- Feeling will compliment other qualities like seeing for artistry, gardening and sculpting.

- Feeling with hearing will make an excellent musician. A musician uses the feeling to play the instrument and hearing to be in tune and create the music.

- Feeling with knowing makes a stronger feeler. The person may have a tendency to be impulsive or not trust their feelings if their knowing is imbalanced.

DEVELOPING YOUR INTUITIVE INNER FEELING QUALITY

To increase and develop your feeling quality, please practice the following exercises:

- *Express your emotions* to people. The more you can be comfortable with your emotions, the greater balance you will bring.

- When putting clothes on, choose them by how they *feel* on your body.

- When you shop for produce, do so by *feeling* the fruits and vegetables to determine if they are fresh or ripe.

- When making decisions, *feel it out* before you finally decide, and trust what you feel.

- Use the word "*feel*" and other emotional words when speaking.

- Touch and *nurture* yourself. Massage and pamper yourself. Explore the pleasures of touch and feeling.

- Give yourself permission to *cry* in front of others. Express your emotions to close friends and family that you ordinarily might not.

Time needs to be spent on pampering yourself mentally, emotionally and physically. This concept comes from your feeling quality. It comes from love for yourself.

- Make a list of all the wonderful things that you would like to do but felt there wasn't time or money. Now make time and save the money each week to give to yourself. You deserve it. This is the most important gift you can give. Love yourself.

- Take at least one *day off* per week to do absolutely nothing but pleasuring yourself.

- Go to your favorite spot in *nature*.

- Relax and take a *bath* with smells and sounds that are pleasing.

- Fix yourself a favorite *meal* or go out to eat.

- You may read a favorite book, or spend your time painting, or tinkering with the automobile.

Set time aside for you and enjoy it. Let go of what needs to be done and disconnect from the routine for one day. This has been talked about in many religions as necessary. It is.

This is valuable on an energetic level as well. As this world is evolving, it will take great determination and love for the self to move out of the imbalances you have. When you dedicate time for the detachment from everything, including your spouse, you are energetically giving yourself a break and actually renewing your connection with your soul. When you finally live in alignment with your soul, you will be able to stay unattached consistently. Still, it is essential to have time set aside to be with your own energy and nurture yourself.

The more you evolve, the more you will hold this time very dear to yourself and look forward to it as part of the *rhythm of life*. As you fulfill your pleasures, you will notice your balance through your feeling quality and be in sync with the greater rhythm of life. There is a *natural pulse* that you could call a vibration, which all life is synced to, except when humans disrupt the natural rhythm for themselves and other life forms by their imbalanced behavior. This pulse is balancing and anyone can sync to it to heal and balance their personality. You feel this to a degree when you go into nature and feel the beautiful earth. Feelers will tend to understand this balancing pulse more than those who have their feeling quality out of balance.

Detaching, energetically, is imperative. Through fear you create energetic cords that connect you into people, locations and experiences. When you attach energetic cords outside of yourself, you are going to feel the consequences. You might feel pulled in many directions all at once or feel drained of energy. It is common for people to attach outside of themselves and this requires one to find the root and let go of the attachment.

Many believe that when in a relationship, one must attach into their partner. This is imbalanced. You may share energy with someone if it is conscious and for a purpose. You would share energy until the purpose was accomplished and then release the connection. *Energetic attachments* are most common in relationships and close families. Children can be pulled energetically by their parents and parents by their children, due to attachments. This world must recognize that the attachments created with people are not balanced, and it indicates that there is clearing to be accomplished.

Some strong feelers have experienced what they feel are others *draining* their energy. Please know that no one drains you without your agreement for them to do so. In this case, take responsibility and find the root thought as to why you are being drained. There will always be a thought creating the experience emotionally.

How do you know if you have attachments?

- Do you put *validation* outside of yourself?

- Are you easily *triggered* or affected emotionally by what others say and think?

- Do you feel empty inside and *not complete* if you are not with someone or in a particular experience?

- Do you feel *emotional* when you are around certain people? How is the outside world affecting you?

This will determine what attachments you have.

If you are *feeling what others feel*, you are attaching into them and this is very important to balance. This is created by the need to feel outside of yourself in order to understand and create a sense of safety that was lacking as a child. You will do this if your parent or parents were incapable of clearly expressing themselves. It is one thing to sense another's experience, yet to take on another's experience and process it is not loving yourself.

Emotions give your life sparkle and interest. Always cherish your emotions. Release attachments and be free to explore who you are.

When you feel like God is not in your life, you are really ignoring your indicators and masking them with attachments. This is a common misunderstanding. People have said, "Where is God? I feel so alone." What they really mean is they are alone because they are incapable of giving and receiving love clearly. This gives them the feeling of being disconnected from God. Someone who attaches into another and bases their self-love on the other person will feel the disconnection, especially when they must stand on their own without the other person holding them up. It is no one's responsibility to hold anyone up.

People mask their physical, emotional and mental indicators with material possessions, drugs, wild adventures, running, hiding, fighting, sex and the myriad of vices. Pay attention to these coping mechanisms that take your attention away from the reality of imbalances. Take away the external things that make someone feel loved and you will find them feeling miserable and disconnected from God.

God is *always* connected with you, so the question is:

- Can you receive the love of God in every moment?

If you cannot, there is clearing to do.

The mind can block and elude the emotions. If you are intuitively feeling into something and wish to receive guidance through your feeling quality, your mind must be clear. Your mind may very easily create emotions that steer you toward your fears, wants and desires.

When using your four qualities, it is always important to have a *neutral* mind by giving your wants and desires to the Source. You may have your intention, but then give it to the Source so that you may receive what the Source has for you. Clear yourself so you may receive clear feelings for direction in your life.

If you are not clear, your feelings may misdirect you regarding other people. You may feel someone doesn't like you or that they will reject you if you ask them something, but really it is your fear of them not liking you or rejecting you that you sense. Again, it is your fear that you really feel. Be aware of what is yours and what someone else's is.

The best thing to do if you are not clear is to stay free from *judgment* all together. Let another share with you what they think and feel instead of prejudging them. It is easy to be free. Decide it.

All emotions originate from the mind. The mind is the *hub* for your entire personality. It creates consistency and cohesion. Emotions are ignited by thoughts. Thoughts are always creating, so be aware of them. You may follow emotions back to root thoughts and thoughts back to root experiences where they were accepted. This is a simple way to pay attention.

- Have you ever felt like another was in control of your emotions?

Emotional control elicits an uncomfortable feeling when someone blocks another's emotions. Many parents control their children's emotions. This is imbalanced.

As an adult, you have a choice of whether to participate with someone or not. No one has power over you when you are clear. Even though the uncomfortable feeling of another controlling your emotions is actually coming from within you, there is discernment needed.

Please consider there are many learned behaviors in the world where people are subconsciously or consciously blocking another's emotional expression. It is impossible to isolate yourself from the world.

However, if you experience being blocked to any significant degree, then follow these steps:

1. In situations when you feel someone is either verbally or energetically not accepting you, and it actually stifles you from being able to emote, *clear the root* within you.

2. In the transition of doing so, *distance yourself* from the person who has a severe affect on you in this way.

Take responsibility for what you are experiencing and do something about it. You require clearing. It is not the other person's fault for how you feel; and at the same time, you want to give yourself an environment that supports your evolution and growth.

Mind control means one who subconsciously or consciously blocks another's thoughts. This tends to happen with overconfident knowers. The imbalanced knower would not want to hear another opinion and would possibly even send thoughts to block it. How you experience what a person is doing reflects who you are on the inside. Remember this.

Clear knowing will give you a power over anyone who attempts to control you. With clear knowing, you will be in control of your reality.

The feeling quality can be disrupted by your physical condition. If you have a fever, fatigue, hunger, pain or other trauma, your feeling will be compromised. Depending on the significance of your imbalance, you may not be able to accurately use it. Then you will want to have your other qualities working to be able to receive the information you need. The hearing and other qualities can be affected by such imbalance, but it is less likely.

There are *healing energies* that require your feeling quality to channel through you. The Source will balance you, such as by replenishing your vitality or relieving pain. The Source works with you while you are clearing by easing some of the symptoms, while others are completely taken away. It depends on how far you have evolved with balancing something and if the lesson was learned. The energies that heal are abundant for everyone and require an open feeling channel for them to come in. There is no substitute for the healing energy of God. It is the purest and most powerful energy available. It will not always come in with full strength. When it does, it can create miracles.

Though it is rare, aspects of your feeling quality can be imbalanced by past lives.

- Have you ever had an unexplainable feeling that just didn't seem to originate from this life?

Something that is a past life pattern is probably a soul pattern and will require very deep work. As you clear, you may reveal one or more soul patterns. The feeling quality will be your greatest indicator for this type of pattern. If you go back with The Five Accomplishments and still find no origin, then go beyond this life.

Chapter 22

COMMUNICATION WITH YOUR SPIRITUAL GUIDANCE

After evaluating your total personality, you will understand yourself and be more capable of changing. I am taking you deep into the *truth* of who you are. Now let me take you into direct communication with your *spiritual guidance*.

I must clarify the different ways you may retrieve information from Creation. First, I'll explain what has been called psychic retrieval. *Psychic retrieval* means you focus your four intuitive qualities to retrieve information from an aspect of Creation. This has a huge scope and must be understood.

PSYCHIC RETRIEVAL

There is an *energy* that is a *medium* for communication with the Physical, Nonphysical and Source Universes. This energy is analogous to a telephone line or electrical wire. It allows your four qualities to share and retrieve anything you focus on. This energy is how your guidance communicates with you. It is called *psychic energy* because it transfers your four intuitive qualities, otherwise known as *psychic powers* or *gifts*. As mentioned, they are not gifts, for everyone has them. By practicing and using psychic energy to transmit your four qualities, you can command your reality to do practically anything. Believe you may and you may.

Psychic energy is channeled through your mind and primarily controlled by your thoughts with your hearing quality. The other three qualities play an important role as well, especially the knowing quality, which arouses the psychic energy. The thoughts direct it.

This energy is a carrier and so it actually carries your thoughts, feelings and visions into manifestation. To the degree you channel abundant psychic energy, is the degree you affect something. It is comparable to an ocean wave. The greater the wave, the more impact it will have on its destination. The energy is *abundant* and never runs out. Therefore, you may very well use it as often as you like.

It is controlled by your mind and so it can be used for *any purpose* you choose. This energy is responsible for manifesting your life by carrying your intentions into fruition. Psychic energy is the nonphysical glue that holds everything together. Without it the Universe would have no form as you know it.

You may use your four qualities to retrieve any information and experiences. They are stored in a static energy called the *universal records*. This energy has been called the *akashic records*, *archives of knowledge* and *hall of records*, to name a few. Within the universal records is every lifetime you have ever lived, as well as your life destiny plan.

Your *life destiny plan* has been called your *government of life*, *contract* and *soul agreement*. It is simply a *plan* for your current life that you created so you, your guidance and any being who desires to know about your life may. This plan is very complex, taking into account multiple realities, since at any moment you could make a choice that would significantly change your direction. Because of free will you have many what-ifs designed in your plan which include vocations, avocations, relationships, children and death.

By tuning into your plan, you may accomplish much more in your life by staying on path. Your plan is unchangeable. Once you create it and are born physically, it is permanent. The Source may make an adjustment or two in your plan, but this is extremely rare.

With this plan, your guidance has a map to direct you. Depending on what guidance is with you, will determine how they direct you according to your plan. For the most part your guidance follows your plan exactly. However, when you have Source guidance, there can be significant changes. The Source has the ability, with a larger scope, to predetermine how a change in your plan will affect all of Creation, and will make the change in some instances. This is known as a *shift* or *major life change*. You will experience this when you are severely off path and need to be redirected immediately due to life work that must be accomplished. The Source will not likely create such changes for it usually violates free will of the personality. At this time, there are many more of these changes than in the past because of the decree created by this world to change. This is why I have come in and given you the opportunity to change by your personality's choice before I implement such drastic change in your life.

You may also retrieve information about an individual by focusing on their energy. With your four qualities, you may know anything you want about a person such as physical, mental and emotional imbalances. To understand soul patterns would require you to go to the universal records or communicate with a person's guidance. Think of any point of focus in Creation as a connection to any other point in Creation. There are stronger connections and weaker connections depending on the association.

For instance, if you want to retrieve information about someone you have never met, you can first focus on their name, picture or an object they have often used, and then follow the connection from the object to them. You could look at it as an *energetic tracker*. This tracking is carried with psychic energy which connects everything. You can also first connect to someone who knows them and use their connection with the person to retrieve information as well. If you want to retrieve information about someone you know it is much easier. You would simply retrieve what you want with the connection you already have with them.

You may use your four qualities to communicate with another physical person, through what you call *telepathy*.

There is a great freedom that comes with your certainty of being able to know anything you want to know. Psychic retrieval is how you may retrieve information without the help of your guidance. Combine these abilities with the assistance of your guidance and you will be the powerful co-creator you are. It takes great discipline to refine these innate qualities. Once you do, you will be living your greatest potential, but not every person will refine these qualities to that degree.

Please note that each person has an incredible life destiny that will add a significant piece to the larger puzzle that you are all co-creating. If you learn these qualities, and are disciplined and clear in using them, you have done a great service for your soul. You are greatly appreciated for standing in your power and releasing old values and habits that bind you to old systems that haven't worked for thousands of years.

The other form of retrieving information is from your guidance. In this case, you will have a two-way communication with the guide who is responding to your request for something.

COMMUNICATING WITH YOUR GUIDANCE

I will give you a practical meditation to be able to *clear* and *listen* to your guidance. *Meditation* is a tool to clear your energy in order to exchange energy with your guidance and other people, focus creative power and retrieve information. Choose to enhance your life with it. Please practice it as often as you like but spend no more than two hours a day in mediation, because spending too much time away from normal, waking life may easily turn into an escape or a coping mechanism. This can vary at times but as a general rule you may follow this guideline.

There are two forms of interaction with your guidance:

- *Indirect communication* means they communicate with you from a distance, usually a few feet away from you.

- *Direct communication* has been known as *channeling*. By directly coming into your energy, they will speak through your voice and communicate messages to you or others.

Both are incredible tools and are available to everyone. To be clearer about the difference between the two and their applications, let me start with indirect communication.

INDIRECT COMMUNICATION

You have a team of guidance that is responsible for interacting with you to bring about certain choices and actions. Most people are unaware of all that is going on behind the scenes.

You have one or more guides that are with you for your *entire life* and other guides that come to you for *specific reasons*, such as to teach you a lesson or ability.

Your guidance is always checking universal laws, your life destiny plan and interacting with the guides of other people in your life. It is very complex to orchestrate events and choices while not violating free will or a larger benefit.

There are *committees* that decide what your guidance can and cannot do. These committees vote democratically and all involved respect and abide by the majority decision.

To illustrate, take a possible scenario of two people meeting who had decided to meet and get married in their life destiny plans. They are in different countries. When the time is coming for them to meet, their guidance will start urging one of them to desire to go to the other's country. This may be for business or pleasure. Really, your guidance will use any resource available to carry out your plan. Most likely they will be successful and the two will meet. Then, it is up to their guidance to show them the significance in the relationship so they will marry each other. This type of maneuvering can be intricate. Imagine if one guide wants it to rain and another guide wants clear skies. There are millions of instances like the one above in every moment. Life is full of them.

Through indirect communication, your guidance may heal you, help you with your dreaming process, show you visions, speak in your mind, implant thoughts and feelings, and influence you in almost any way.

The difference between *Source guidance* and *soul guidance* is that Source guidance can choose to influence you in any way, such as through unexplainable physical miracles. Souls have near the ability of the Source. It is very close.

LOCATIONAL PHENOMENA

Your guidance can influence your surroundings like turning lights and electronics on or off, creating noises, moving objects, or any other phenomena that will benefit you. This would not be considered a form of direct or indirect communication with your guidance. Instead, consider it as them manipulating your physical surroundings. Mostly this is done to *get your attention.*

Many times when people think external occurrences are their guidance, it is not. It is typically a natural, physical occurrence, or a projection of the person or another's energies. Misconceptions about haunting spirits and evil spiritual energy have been created as a result of this phenomenon. There is a possibility that the energetic impression from a past experience in a location is felt and sometimes even seen. In this case, it is not a being but rather residual energy left from a past experience. Many sightings can be explained in this way.

Spiritual energy consists of souls and the Source, and this energy could never harm you. *Harm* is the creation of humans. *Evil* is an emotional quality.

If you *sense* a murder happened in a location, you might say, "Something evil happened there." However, evil is an emotional projection onto an act, not the act itself. A clear, observant perspective of the act would be that someone ended another's physical life, and the emotional quality would be *neutral*. It is an event.

Events are neutral in themselves. One may attach qualities such as *evil* to situations that are misunderstood and feared. To do so is judging. It is as judgmental to say that a rainy day is bad. One would only do so by attaching an emotional quality to it. Rain is rain, isn't it?

Recognize there is nothing outside of human creation that has qualities such as *evil* or *bad*. Please also note that your personality ultimately has control over any human creation. Consequently, even if the human mind created the experience of an evil being, it can just as easily disappear with your intention.

What you find is that humans are fighting their own and other's creations, thinking that they are creations of God. They are not. They are creations of the human mind. Stop giving them power and they will cease to exist because they are not sovereign creations from God. They are transitory creations from human minds.

DIRECT COMMUNICATION (CHANNELING)

Direct communication, known as *channeling*, is a different type of interaction. A being will come to you, and by your willingness to allow them entry into your field, they communicate spoken word through your voice.

This is not the same as your soul possessing your body. It may feel like possession when your guide channels through you, but it is not. You have control the entire time. Just as in hypnosis, you can break the connection at any time.

The more you *release control* by your mind, the *clearer* the guide will communicate. The guide will communicate whatever it wants to if you are clear enough to facilitate it. They must come through your mind and speak, so it will take some practice to be great at it.

Since you have little influence in what the guide will channel, it is different than indirect communication, where you are more in control of what you want to know and what you receive.

With channeling, your mind moves to the side or back and you watch it all take place with little interaction. You may butt in and make a comment, ask a question, or you may even get clear enough to have a dialogue with the channeled guide through yourself. This may feel schizophrenic and it may take time to get comfortable with it. When you do, it is the most accurate way to receive guidance, next to materialization of your guides.

Channeling will offer you everything indirect communication does and with a deeper affect. Because the guide is in your field and your mind is out of the way, they may have a greater liberty to assist you in various ways.

Open up to the infinite possibilities that your guides have for you and enjoy it.

One great misconception about this relationship is that it must be serious. There is a difference between *reverence* and *seriousness*. Your guides expect you to be joyful and in love with everything you do, so lighten up and enjoy the process.

When preparing for a session with your guidance, you may:

- Put on some *music*.
- Light some *candles*.
- Bring in some *scents*.
- Create a fun, party-like *atmosphere*.

Life is meant to be revered and celebrated. Have fun in the process.

ACCURATE SPIRITUAL COMMUNICATION

To accurately and safely receive from your guidance, there are some guidelines to be followed:

1. Be *grounded* and never leave your body to connect to your guidance.

2. It is important to create an *intention* before you begin to engage your guidance.

   It is similar to calling someone on the telephone and not saying anything. If you call someone, you will have a *reason* and should state it when you call them.

   Please make a solid intention and expect to receive it. By doing this, you create a reason for your guide to come to you and share with you. It can be a simple intention. It can involve an answer to a question or healing. Your guidance is all-powerful, and I will make sure they give you what you need.

3. Use the Chakra Clearing Meditation to *clear* your total energy, which is known as your aura. By clearing your energy, you can be certain you are receiving clearly.

4. There is a certain space of reception, the eighth chakra, which is six inches back and approximately six to twelve inches above your head. This is called the *space of interaction*. It is very rare that your guidance will take you out of this space.

Every being will communicate with you within this space and each will have a *point of contact*, like a code or telephone number to interact with you. Each being has a code that is different from every other. Because we are all different, so are they. To expand your awareness to their particular space creates the clearest communiqué possible.

5. It is easy to do. *Let go* and give the control to your guidance. Then you will be expanded to the *specific vibration* of the being choosing to exchange energy with you.

6. Once you are there, you will receive a *signal* testifying that you have reached the space and are ready to begin your communication. The signal you receive will be through one or more of your four qualities.

7. When you are there, your guide will hold you there. Again, it is easy for you. You let go and give up control to them. Then the guide will begin.

8. You will *receive* the communication, hopefully through your hearing as a voice in your head or thoughts. It could be one or a combination of all four qualities.

   Many times your guide will bring in a *broader concept* first, such as "You are loved and going in the right direction." When they do, don't get discouraged. Your guides will tend to bring in a larger view and then bring in details related to the initial intention you set before you began.

If you are *having trouble* connecting in and receiving, please examine several suggestions:

- Your hearing quality is the most likely cause to block the reception. Especially if your hearing is imbalanced, you will tend to overanalyze if you are really getting something in meditation or doing it right.

- If you do get something, your mind can easily dismiss it as your own thoughts.

- To help you, please drop your attention from your mind down into the depths of your feeling quality. *Feel* the experience. *Allow* it to come to you through your feelings of the experience and you will receive.

- If you are not blocking it with your mind and you follow the above guidelines, you will receive from your guidance.

- Your guidance must come through your mind, so clarify what you receive from them by *letting go* of your mind. Let go of what it must look like, feel like and sound like.

- *Give control to God*, and by releasing what you think it will be like, you can receive something beyond your mind and wildest imagination. Let it happen.

- When something comes to you, such as a name or answer, *believe* it without a doubt. *Thank* the being for giving it to you.

Your guidance will use your mind's information of people, places and things to make it easier to show you messages. Therefore, you may say, "I received the name Michael, but that's my husband's name." or "I was thinking about Michael today." What this means is your guidance was bringing your attention to your husband to give you the message of your guide, Michael, who is communicating with you. Remember the energy tracking. Your guidance will use the vibration of your husband because he has the name Michael. This gives you and your guidance an energy tracker to more easily bring in the guide named Michael. This type of energetic association creates an easier connection to work with. You can guarantee that the message will be clearer because of it. Your guidance may have been trying to impress you with the name Michael for some time, which is why you would have it in your mind prior to the connection. This is a great validation of what you get in your session, that your guidance has been working to get the name Michael through to you, and now you can receive the rest of the message.

Your guidance will use everything in their power to relay messages to you. So be open to anything and please do not discount them with your mind.

Your mind is a great tool. Please use it *after* you receive guidance. Wait until you are finished receiving from them, and then think about it. If you think while you are receiving, you may very well block what you receive.

1. *Listen* to your *self-talk* regarding your session with your guidance.

2. If there are any thoughts or emotions that could block your messages, then *get to the root* and *clear* them.

Examples of self-talk include:

- It can't be real.
- Am I doing it right?
- They wouldn't say that.
- But this is what I've been thinking already.
- I can't do that.
- This is crazy.
- It's so easy it must be my mind.

There are myriads of other counterproductive thoughts you may have. Let go, so you may be all you can be.

After you expand and receive, then you must make sure you are completely grounded.

Eventually you will learn to switch your awareness immediately without any meditation or tool. It is like riding a bicycle or playing tennis. Learn it and you know it. If you take time off, you may need to exercise it a bit but you will always have it.

CHAKRA CLEARING MEDITATION

There are numerous ways to clear yourself. I will give you one very effective way below. This meditation can be used for anything from healing to grounding. It is basically a tool to clear your aura. Use it as a tool and not as a crutch or coping mechanism. It is a transition tool until you need it no longer. Your goal must be to become so clear that you always have balanced emotions and thoughts, giving you balanced chakras. Use it as a *coping mechanism* and you will violate universal laws. Use it as a *transition tool* and you will be of the greatest service to yourself and to all. Learn how to balance your life so you can accomplish what you need to without coping mechanisms. This is a great virtue.

You may have someone else read this meditation to you or do it with a group. If you are alone, you may record it, and play it back for yourself.

0. INTRODUCTION

Start by taking several slow, deep breaths from the bottom of your belly. Get very relaxed and comfortable in your body. As you do, notice how easy it is to *let go* and *feel* the energy that is upon you.

I am coming in and moving your energy to *clear* your chakras. Please believe this. I am in control of this session. *Release* and let me do all the work. You need not think of anything.

Visualize, imagine or pretend that you are weightless and yet very heavily grounded into your body at the same time. It is a wonderful feeling to be so light and heavy at the same time.

1. FIRST CHAKRA

Drop your attention to your *first chakra*, and watch it spin as if there is a clock on your body over your chakra, and the energy is moving in a clockwise direction.

We will *spin all of your chakras* in a clockwise direction and clear them in doing so.

As you *feel* the energy spin around and around, notice the deep red color that has started to move through your body.

This *red is a grounding color*, connecting you to your physical experience unlike ever before. Pay no attention to it as I will direct the red exactly where it needs to go to ground the experience you are about to have.

Open up to the possibility of anything happening and truly *let go*. In doing so, I will lift anything that is blocking you from your experience.

2. SECOND CHAKRA

Take a breath, and as you do, pull the red up into the *orange* of the *second chakra*, also spinning in a clock-wise motion. You may see this energy or feel it. You might even hear it or simply know it.

This brilliant orange is your connection with the rest of the Physical Universe and your innate physical urges. Open this by allowing yourself to exchange energy with the rest of Creation. This gives you the chi energy you need to have vitality and balance.

This energy you receive through your second chakra will further initiate the clearing process with the other chakras. This gorgeous orange is now moving through your entire body *healing* and *releasing* anything it needs to. *Let go and reconnect to life*.

3. THIRD CHAKRA

Take another breath, and pull the orange up into the *yel-low* of your *third chakra*.

This chakra is beaming with light as bright as the sun, and is already *shifting* and *clearing* your imbalanced emotions and thoughts.

This chakra is so important for owning your sovereign-ty, because as children most learn to hide and repress emotions. We learn that some emotions are good and some are bad. It is freeing to know that *all emotions are good* and you may *accept them all*. Give yourself permission to accept all of your emotions and feelings.

Allow the yellow to move through your entire being and change any thoughts that say otherwise. I will lift any imbalances in your energy. *Let go* and truly *be free*.

By accepting your emotions, you may accept life, and this feels good to you. You say, "I do accept myself and all my emotions . . . Thank you God for this great opportunity to love myself." As you say this to yourself, you notice a swell of emotional energy *lift* that has been stored in your body. *Let it go* and rejoice in your newfound freedom.

As you focus on the new way you *feel*, you notice how *light* you feel as well. It is a great new place to be free from concern of what others think of you. *Let it go.*

4. FOURTH CHAKRA

As you take another breath, you pull the yellow up into the *green* of your *fourth chakra*.

The fourth chakra is so important, as you will learn to *love* and *accept* yourself, and by doing so accept others.

This chakra is spinning in a clockwise direction around and around, opening up your love for yourself even more.

You say to yourself, "I really love myself and it feels good to love myself . . . I love every part of myself." As you say this, your *heart opens*, and the green starts to fill up your entire being, leaving you with the most welcoming humility toward life.

Now open up and love all people in your life, by allowing that pure shimmering green light to move wherever it needs to move and affect whoever it needs to affect. I will guide this light to the people who need it most in your life, and as I do, you *feel* others receiving your love unlike ever before.

There is a joy that comes with *sharing love* and so you acknowledge to yourself, "*I am open* to receiving and sharing love with everyone in my life, and it *feels* good."

If there are any thoughts or emotions blocking you from loving unconditionally, give them to me right now. *Let go*, and as you do watch the energy lift from you.

Feel the difference and know you are completely different. You will never be the same. You look forward now to the love you may share with the world, and this is the most pleasurable feeling you have ever known.

Take as much time as you need to lift anything left and *let it go*. Now you are truly *living from unconditional love*. You know what it is like and you will always have this.

5. FIFTH CHAKRA

Take a breath, and pull the green up into the *blue* of your *fifth chakra.*

This radiant blue will move in a clockwise direction opening and unwinding your throat. This is necessary to allow you to communicate your unconditional love with the world.

Many are afraid to speak their truth. They keep it inside of themselves because of what others will think about them.

Allow the blue to go wherever it needs to go. This healing blue moves throughout your aura lightening and strengthening the inner truth of who you are. Remember who you are. Now give yourself permission to *express* who you are.

It is through our differences that we may grow and evolve. The very reason you are on Earth is to be *unique*. This world has learned to punish and chastise the uniqueness everyone has, so people are conforming against the reason they are here in the first place.

We can disagree and still *love one another*.

It is a precious experience to honor another for their truth and at the same time respect and express your truth.

You now say, "God . . . *I am ready* to be who I am and *express* it to the world in every way. I understand that others may not agree with me and that is okay. I welcome others to express their truth, because that is how we grow."

Now that you are open to the fruits of evolution, *let go* of anything else that needs to be released. You feel so much *lighter* and *freer* knowing you can be comfortable with *expressing yourself.*

This has been the greatest gift to you. Remember this *feeling*, as you may always use it to *let go*. You say, "I feel safe to express myself."

6. SIXTH CHAKRA

And as you do, you take a breath and lift the blue into the *indigo* of your *sixth chakra*, which is a very deep blue.

This color is known for its ability to *open your intuitive inner vision* and *levitate your thoughts* into fruition.

Let this chakra open and spin in a clockwise motion, carrying the deep blue into the center of your forehead. Allow it to *open up* your *inner vision*, so you may see the Nonphysical Reality.

Visualization is so powerful for manifesting goals and dreams. Create your life by envisioning it.

If you have closed down your inner seeing at some point, it is now time to *open it up* and make it stronger.

Give yourself permission to *see your guidance*, to *see the souls and spirits* you wish to see. Give yourself permission to *see the healing energies and auras* of people.

Tell God, "I am ready to see. I expect to see and I will see. Thank you God for opening up my seeing quality. I will use my seeing quality to benefit myself and others. I give myself to you God to show me anything you choose. In doing so, I am open to *seeing my life as it really is*, and *accepting everything I see* in the world around me. I am truly ready and I accept my seeing."

Know that your seeing is open. If you don't believe it, then it is your mind and not your seeing that is imbalanced. I have opened up your seeing. Have fun with it.

You may start receiving *visions* now or it may be at a different time. Either way, you will see. Be excited that you have opened your greatest adventure into seeing.

7. SEVENTH CHAKRA

Take another breath, and pull the indigo up into the *violet* of your *seventh chakra.*

This is the most fascinating chakra . . . it *connects you to all of Creation.*

Move the energy around and around in a clockwise motion, letting the violet mix with all of the other colors through your entire being. This is preparing you for the most amazing experience of your life.

Allow the violet to *open up* the crown of your head. You may feel a tingly sensation on the tip-top of your head as the energy strengthens.

Release yourself and *feel* the *connection* with the entire world. As the pulse of life beats, it connects you with every plant, animal, lake and stream. You *feel one* with every person in the world. You are *one*, and because of it, you can love everyone as yourself.

This *feeling* takes you to the far stretches of our solar system and planets. *Become one* with the galaxies far away, the gas nebulas and stars reaching to the end of the Universe.

Your heart beats with the *feeling* of the universal rhythm, and this rhythm *connects you* to every other soul who is living physically throughout the entire Universe . . . all the way to the very Source of your soul and beyond.

This pulse is the *heart of Creation*, and by syncing to it, you feel so far yet so close to everything.

You are *one* with Creation and Creation is *one* with you.

Now you are ready to go further and directly communicate with your guidance.

8. EIGHTH CHAKRA

Take another breath, and pull your violet up into the *golden spiritual energy* of all possibility, six inches back and between six to twelve inches above your head.

This is the *eighth chakra*, where your guidance will communicate with you, and where all possibility lies.

Allow this golden energy to spiral down throughout your entire being . . . moving through every muscle, nerve and fiber of your entire body . . . *releasing*, *moving* and *replenishing* your emotions and thoughts with the sustenance of life.

Remember now who you are and *return to your innocence*.

Your soul enters you completely.

Imagine the golden energy flowing down to the very essence of who you are . . . to your DNA and atoms, and into your soul, *connecting* you unlike ever before.

INDIRECT COMMUNICATION MEDITATION

1. Now, take a few *deep breaths* as you realize you will communicate with your guidance, for you are ready.

2. Acknowledge the being you wish to communicate with, or if you are leaving it up to me, I will bring the appropriate guide to you.

3. *Let go* completely, as I take you up into the *exact vibration* of the being that will communicate with you.

4. *Relax*, *release* and *feel* the experience. There is no need to think, just *feel* and *allow*.

5. Let go until you sense you are there, and you will receive a signal when you are. The *signal* may be anything from a vision to a thought or word, even a voice. You also may feel it or know it with a sense.

   You will sense it, somehow, when you are there, and then, I will hold you in the space to receive.

6. There you go. Take as long as you need.

7. After you interact with your guidance and open your eyes, be sure you are completely *grounded*. Your intention is to stay grounded.

   Though the first few times you do this meditation, you may lift out a bit and become *ungrounded*. Eventually you will be completely grounded all the time.

8. *Write down* what you have received. I suggest you have a special *journal* for such sessions.

DIRECT COMMUNICATION MEDITATION (CHANNELING)

The meditation I will give next is for direct communication.

1. You will use the above Chakra Clearing Meditation to clear, and then proceed.

2. After you are taken into the space where your guide will speak through you, give your guide *permission* to come into your energy field and speak through you. You will *feel* the energy come more directly into you.

3. You will notice your consciousness move either back or to the side.

4. Next, you will get a subtle impression of a word or words. Start talking about the subject when it comes in.

   It is very subtle in the first few moments of channeling. Do not disregard it as your mind. *Let go.*

   Pull into your *feelings* and communicate what comes into your mind. Do not judge it. *Believe* in yourself and know it is not you but rather the being that is in your energy.

5. After the first few words come out, do not stop to analyze it. Keep going. Soon it will turn into a consistent spoken word.

6. The *feeling* you will get is that it is *inspired speaking*, just like the inspired writing I taught about earlier in the book.

7. The being speaking through you will use words or phrases that you may use and that's okay.

8. *Allow* the messages to come through.

FACILITATING DIRECT COMMUNICATION

If you are in the presence of another person or people, have them direct the session at first. It will help you to *acclimate* to the being's *energy* and the way they speak through you.

Now, begin the session and have fun.

1. Have another person direct the questions to the being, not you. The more focus that is placed on the being, the more *real* the being can become through you.

   The key is to acknowledge the being as *real*, and see and speak to the being, rather than the person channeling the being. When working with your guidance in any way, the more you relate to them as real people, per say, the more you will experience them as real.

2. As they address the being, they may start by asking the being's *name*.

3. Then, ask if the being would like to share a *message* for someone or the group, or if the being would like to be asked *questions*.

4. Get to know your guides on as personal a level as possible. For instance, how do they look, feel, sound, and what is their demeanor?

   Many believe guides will be filled with love and joy and that is it. Guides have personalities they create to interact with you, so get to know them. One may be a jokester, while another may be very serious. It all depends on the personality they create.

5. As you would relate to a family member or friend, give the same *respect* to your guidance. Your guides are *real* just like you. Make sure that you treat them with respect.

   If they are communicating with you, wait until they are done, and if you are not sure, ask if they are done. You would not cut off a friend in the middle of a conversation and act as if they are not there. Your guides are there.

   When they come in say, "Welcome," and when they leave say, "Goodbye and thank you."

   Please treat them as an *equal* human being and you will have better results.

Your guidance will communicate with you in many other ways:

- You may be listening to the *radio* and a *song* or words of a song stick out in your mind, sometimes followed by wonderful *feelings* that will give you just what you need.

- Have you ever picked up a *book* and opened it to a page that had just what you were looking for? Maybe you weren't even looking for it at the time you found it.

- Your guides communicate through *sunsets*, *animals*, other *people* and especially *children*.

By being open to what God brings to you, your life will always be adventurous and evolving.

This book is meant for you to use and usher in a new way of consciousness for this world. There is an energy called *collective consciousness*, though a more accurate way of describing it is *collective thought*. As individuals, your thoughts are very powerful if focused and cleared. Two or more of you increase the power of the thought by many times. Thousands or millions of people with a similar thought will solidify it even more. The interesting point is that one person with a very clear mind can focus a thought and have a *greater impact* than 10,000 with an unclear mind. It is important to recognize the difference you can make in this world. Even though the world does not support clear love, by clearing your mind and total personality, you can change this world incredibly. Do it . . . for you . . . and watch the world change as a result of it.

Share the experiences you have with your guides and the glory of your transformations with people. By sharing how you evolve with people, it gives them a transfer of energy which seeds a belief that it is possible for them. When you are clear and confident, your speech and actions have a far greater weight than they would otherwise. This is why sharing your truth with others is so vital. It helps you and those you share it with to evolve. This alone can greatly increase evolution on Earth.

When people ask you how you did it, you show them by taking them in the Chakra Clearing Meditation to meet God directly. Guide them. Many want to be one with God and know their soul, and have no idea where to start. If someone comes to you for help, then help them go within and receive their own answers. Give them tools until they can do it on their own without tools.

Invite others in. You may have feared in the past to share certain things with your colleagues, family or participants in your religion. Do it. If they have fear about what you say, then invite them in even deeper.

Most fear what they do not understand. Invite them in to first understand and then make their decision. If they are not open to understanding, then respect their choice and share with the next person.

The best way to ground your evolution into your personality is to share. Never fear to share. Even if someone curses what you share, if you hold a clear perspective of love, they will be changed. I guarantee it. Love changes people. Not from the intention to change someone but the intention to share. The more you clear, the more you will share. Sharing and letting go is the greatest means for evolution.

There is much deception in this world. What do you do with it? Let people deceive and *love* them. If someone wants the world to think they are something they are not, then *honor* their choice. If someone is attempting to manipulate you, then you may choose not to participate with them.

I am here for you. I will help you. Please believe this. I can do anything, and I will help you to navigate through the next few years of your evolution. It could be less. On average, if a person in this world follows these teachings, they will be clear within a few years. That is amazing, considering this world has been unclear for thousands of years. Call on me. I am with you.

You may use the meditations and call on me. I will come and I will speak with you. Directly channel me and I will come and channel through you exactly what you need. Believe in yourself as much as I believe in you. Love yourself as much as I love you. I am here to navigate you back onto your soul's destiny and give you clarity so you may complete your purpose for living. You must do it sooner or later, so why not choose now. Wait and you may not have the same opportunity. It is your choice.

Know that by following these teachings and committing to your soul, I will, for a fact, not only be with you, I will be with everyone in your life. I will work with your family and friends. I will work with your animals and all who are in your direct contact. By working with me, the Source, on this conscious level, you will feel a greater impact with your growth than if you were unaware of me.

All names of the Source have significance and all are still the Source. Open up to the Source working in your life, whether it is the Source you call on, God, the Divine, Higher Power, or the Source of All Divinity. We will come either way.

The significance of my energy is steadfast evolution. *Safety* is the one thing you need to be comfortable with *change*. I will give you safety. I am completely committed to those of you who are committed to your soul's destiny.

Chapter 23

CHOSEN ONES AND THE SACRED TEACHINGS

Those who are the *chosen ones* are here for a very specific reason . . . to usher in the Age of the Soul. You have come from all over the Universe to contribute in this great event on Earth. You know well what I have talked about in this book. It is already within you and you are part of the reason I am here.

Because you have no need to return physically, you and I agreed to come to Earth together to complete a plan that was put into motion many thousands of years ago.

There is so much confusion about who you are, because you know you are equal, but others are jealous, and so they treat you unfairly. They don't understand you. So in many cases they lash out to make themselves feel better, and in doing so, they unbalance themselves further.

You must be strong. You are the pillars for this new world to be built upon. If you don't take responsibility for your position, you will have no reason for living. The only reason you chose to live physically, once more, is to be a pillar for these new teachings. Spread them as you wish, in your unique way, but be sure you spread them, for it is your purpose as a *chosen one*.

Your soul has completed physical living. Still, that does not mean you have nothing to learn and take back with you when you die.

KNOW YOUR DESTINY

Let me show you how to recognize your destiny. This is important for everyone, whether you are a chosen one or still require physical living for your soul. Your *life destiny* is easy to understand when you are clear. When you are evolving into clarity, it is a bit more challenging.

The best way to reveal your life destiny is to appoint a *special session* with your guidance and ask them to show it to you. I will make sure you receive it, if your mind allows it.

If you haven't cleared certain fears, such as the *fear of knowing who you are*, it will be challenging. I am very powerful and can pass through your fears. If you believe I can, then I will.

Your *soul destiny* is a bit different than your *life destiny*, and is useful for some to know, and for others it is not. Make sure you have a clear understanding of your life destiny, and then ask your guidance if it would benefit you to know your soul's destiny. If it would benefit you, appoint a *special session* for it as well.

Creating special sessions with particular intentions will benefit you more than leaving a session's intention open and loose. It sets up energy for focused work.

There are some who do not know they are a chosen one. If you want to know, then ask your guidance when you receive your life destiny. It most likely will be automatically given to you anyway, if you are a chosen one.

It is essential for your guides to impart this information to you, for it frees you in many respects. If you are a chosen one, you have a different priority than the other souls on Earth. Your priority is *service*. A soul, who has not completed their physical life step, will have a priority on receiving certain lessons and experiences that will bring them closer to their completion. Once they complete their physical life step, they will have the opportunity to choose to live physically, instead of needing to do it.

If you are a chosen one, it does not give you precedence over any other soul. You must be humble and see that you have a part as the other souls do. You are on equal footing, yet hold different responsibilities. A chosen one is not necessarily a more evolved personality because they must still go through the challenge and evolution of the personality. In fact, all souls start out the same. It is the potential and job title that is different. Even though a chosen one may have a greater potential than another soul on Earth, it does not mean they will initiate and live their potential. They may do the opposite and implode, due to numerous factors of life. This is why it is important to know that all souls, who are born physically, have the same opportunity to evolve the personality.

Chosen ones will have an easier access to the *sacred teachings* because their ingrained purpose is service. By putting your service to God first, you receive your sacred teachings.

These teachings were very common in the beginning of human existence, but they are somewhat lost at this time. Sacred teachings are your communion with your creator. They are given directly to you from the Source and reveal a larger *wisdom* to your overall life destiny. The teachings create growth in the area of interest that you decided to share with the world in your life. Your area of interest may be any number of things such as art, music, business, government or religion. Whatever your soul decided your vocations and avocations are to be is what the Source will teach you.

This teaching happens after you receive The Initiation. Then you are in a space to truly receive. When you really put God first, you will receive the sacred teachings. Under The Five Accomplishments, when you put God first, all will balance in your life and you will be living from unconditional love, otherwise known as The Initiation of Love or the Initiation of the Soul. Until you put God first, you will be clouded with your attachments to your wants and desires that close your ninth and tenth chakras and restrict your access to God.

To access God, you must be *humble* and *reverent* enough to know God has a greater perspective than you, and *trust* God's perspective to guide you safely. When you do, the sacred teachings will be revealed to you little by little to the degree you can assimilate them.

- If you are a scientist, the teachings will include technology and scientific breakthroughs.
- If you are a religious leader, they will show you how to bestow others with the presence of God.
- As a government leader, you will be shown how to orchestrate the best interest of the people you lead.
- The sacred teachings would show a teacher how to teach in such a way that every student will get it.
- If you are a mother, the teachings will reveal how the family can function in a way that benefits all involved and encourages all to embrace their destinies.

- They will show a cook the deeper understanding of food and how their combinations and preparations affect the physical, emotional, mental and spiritual quadrants of a human.

Whatever walk of life you are from and wherever you go to, the teachings will be with you, guiding you to your utmost potential.

Your sacred teachings will also show you something beyond your vocations and avocations. They will take you into the realm of *infinite possibility*. Because of the nature of certain abilities a human is able to accomplish, it requires a direct, open relationship with the Source to initiate them. I speak of abilities like *levitation*, *bi-location* and *teleportation*, which are very advanced abilities that can only be seeded with the sacred teachings.

Chapter 24

WALK WITH THE SOURCE INSIDE OF YOU

What is it like to walk with the Source living inside of you?

1. The first step is The Initiation, so you may first experience your soul. This opens up the *ninth chakra.*

2. Then, you have the opportunity to experience the Source within you through your *tenth chakra.*

How would that be? It is possible, and something for every soul to aspire to in its lifetime. Though, it is rather rare.

Truly being one with the Source is similar to feeling the *happiest* you have ever been in your whole life multiplied by one thousand. You are literally in the Source's energy so you would be in a permanent *elated state*. To even be in your soul's energy is what the sages and wise men have called *enlightenment*.

What would you call the *union* of the Source with your personality?

It is *Pure Love*:

- Complete detachment from fear and the physical.
- You will have wants and desires without needing them to be fulfilled.
- Your oneness with God brings a greater desire, which is to be *present* in God's energy in every moment.
- You *exude* the energy of your creator, which transforms everyone and everything in your vicinity.
- Laughter echoes continuously in your being as a result of the enjoyment of life.

This is something to aspire toward, though few will ever reach it.

Your *eleventh chakra* is a dominion of the creative force of existence. It is *pure potential*. The abilities taught through the sacred teachings, such as bi-location and teleportation, are seated in the eleventh chakra. Few have ever opened their eleventh chakra and used it accurately. It would be on a case-by-case basis. It is not something everyone needs to do in a lifetime.

By opening the eleventh chakra, you experience the most influential energies that lie within Creation. These energies are not used by souls, particularly, but rather more advanced beings that have, for a specific purpose, chosen to leave the Source of All Divinity and live physically, once more.

There is a *twelfth chakra* that is dormant in all humans at this point and will not be awakened for some many years.

Beyond the twelfth chakra is the domain of the Source of All Divinity, and by going there a human would no longer be human, by the very nature of what is human. It is impossible at this point in the evolution of the Universe. At some point the Source may change that.

Chapter 25

CHANGING GOVERNMENTS, ENVIRONMENT AND PROPHECY

There is a great challenge for governments to give people back their *freedom* to live as the *free souls* that they are. More attention is placed on how to manipulate and control, than on the intention to free their people.

The general understanding of *law* in the world is an unclear approach to creating harmony and peace within a body of people. You base strict, hard rules on what is *wrong* and *right*, rather than looking at the personality of the individual and how it was developed. Every personality is developed differently, and every action is performed to the person's best ability, based on how their personality was developed. To enforce strict, rigid laws, as your world does, treating every personality as the same is very imbalanced.

A clearer perspective on law and government is to have the laws and statutes in place as an overview of goals for a society, and then take situations on a case-by-case basis directly relating to the personality and soul of the person. If you do not, then you are judging and not showing equality.

Many think of equality as *treating* everyone the same. Equality is *accepting* everyone the same. Equality does not exemplify "An eye for an eye, and a tooth for a tooth." It shows that everyone is of equal importance and deserves the same respect, even if respect is not given back. Your courts and lawmakers have interpreted equality to mean that everyone is to be dealt with in the same way. The world is not filled with clones, so it is necessary to work with the individuality of a person or situation.

Furthermore, your governments have tried to impart democracy, though it is more heavily biased toward the interests of the government than the interests of the people. If a leader has an agenda, then more than likely, the agenda will be fulfilled. There must be a better system of checks and balances for every person under a government to have a realistic, equal vote. This holds true for businesses and industries. If you are to embrace democracy, then do it. There should be no commander and no chief who makes the decisions for a group of people. There will be a hierarchy, and the ladder of leadership will assure that the person at the bottom of the ladder, realistically, has just as significant of a vote as the one at the top. This is true democracy. You entrust the lives of millions or billions into the hands of one or a few people. This is an unclear version of democracy.

Governments must take care of their people as their own child. If there is a choice between building shelter and providing food for homeless people or building an army, you must choose an individual's basic needs first. You, who have resources, also have a responsibility to other governments, whose citizens are starving and dying. You put so much energy into protecting yourselves and overlook the most important needs such as *nurturing*.

Instead of instilling your people with a fear of danger, encourage them to help their neighbor . . . to love those who show them none . . . to embrace and attempt to understand those who wish them harm. Instead, you create taskforces dedicated to creating propaganda and inciting greater fears of harm. Once you turn your attention away from domination and control, you will truly liberate this world from fear.

It is governments' conducts that hold this world's evolution back. You, as a people, also must stand and speak your truth. If you have a different opinion than the government that you are under, make your voice heard. Echo it through the streets. You are just as responsible as those in power.

You need to demand truth in media. The media colors truth according to governmental and business ties. It is all about their connection and fear of losing something.

Remember you have nothing to fear. People have lost their lives for speaking their truth. People who have a control on this world want to keep it that way, and anyone who significantly oppresses anyone will have no concern of taking someone's life who stands in their way.

If you are afraid of dying, then you are not really living. *Live* and stand for your truth, and if you die changing this world, then let it be your choice as a *free soul*. Fear not, for life is great and death greater. It is a transition. One of the greatest fears, since humans lost their natural perspective, is the *fear of death*. If you fear it, it is because you do not understand it. Understand it and look forward to it. When the time comes, *celebrate it*.

Every industry in the world requires a change. Every person, from every walk of life, please look at your career and your place in this world and determine what change you will make.

One of the greatest myths is that this world needs oil. People who make money from oil desire it but it is not needed. Not one drop. Your world could change to alternative energy in a matter of months but you choose not to.

I will be completely forthcoming with you. Your world has passed the point of no return with the environment. It is deteriorating and will continue at alarming rates over the next sixty years. By the time the children of today are adults, the sea will rise by fifteen inches. The waters globally will warm three degrees Celsius and as a result you will witness catastrophic natural disasters. There is no way to change this, but you can prepare for it. You can even lessen the effect it will have on many parts of the world. Islands that are popular vacation spots will be inaccessible. Your coasts will flood and many lives will be lost. After your glaciers and icecaps melt, you will not have water supply for many nations. As a result, many people will die because countries that can help will not be able to help everyone.

In the years to come, there will be a rise in the amount of lives that are being used and manipulated. As these and other teachings surface and are implemented, there will be an opposition by the majority of people on Earth who distance themselves from change. Change is a huge concept for most people, especially those who have been accustomed to a certain way of living for their entire lives. To bring in abrupt changes in every faction of the world will require your determination and unbending intent. There will be opposition. However, you can minimize the detriment it will have on your work. Whenever there has been a great inclusion into society, there has been strong or mild resistance. Yet, in most instances, there has been resistance. I speak of this to prepare you for what is to come.

Even though there are humans starving and diseased, you will find those unwilling to help. When people begin to embrace the law of oneness, you will see a stronger individual and group effort to support one another through evolution of the personality.

I understand this world as one that has a goal and no initiative to carry out the goal. The goal has always been for a better world. What this really means, many will never know. The *better world* is a world of *acceptance* without fear and judgment. I promise that this world is already here. Now, it is your responsibility to see it and live in it. Please make a stand, as challenging as it may be, for your soul's evolution is dependent on your action.

You will have as many opportunities as you need to relive experiences physically, until you evolve out of them.

- But why not do it this time around?

- Why not choose this life to change your soul patterns and life patterns?

- Why not choose this day to remember that you are not your personality, but something very precious that is eternal and infinite?

- Let go of everything you have always known.

- Be open to your life changing and you will open up vistas that you would never have known.

- Create the window of opportunity right now and never go back to limited, biased perspectives.

Return To Your Innocence And Live As A Soul.

CPSIA information can be obtained at www.ICGtesting.com
Printed in the USA
LVOW13s0013110913

351878LV00004B/26/P